CROSS COUNTRY
AND ALL THAT STUFF

PETER HEMMING

Copyright ©2022 Peter Hemming

The right of Peter Hemming to be identified as the Author of the Work has been asserted by him in accordance with the Copyright, Designs and Patents Act 1988

All rights reserved. No part of this publication may be reproduced, stored in a retrieval system, or transmitted in any form or by any means without prior written permission of the author, nor be otherwise circulated in any form of binding or cover other than that in which it is published and without a similar condition being imposed on the subsequent purchaser.

Cover photo: Courtesy of Linsey Wraith

www.abrushwithpaint.co.uk

ISBN: 9798364105424

THANKS

To dedicate or acknowledge? That is the question. The answer is neither, thank you is enough so I'll start at the beginning, by thanking the youngster on the front cover.

Thank you Thomas: I know you didn't mean to lose your spikes in the mud at Aykley Heads but amazingly you didn't give up, carrying them, and yourself, on to finish the race. You've earned your place on the front cover.

Thank you to my club mates, past and present. Over the years we shared the mud, sweat, tears and pain of cross country running which ultimately lead to post race banter and the exhilaration of a hot shower.

Thank you juniors: especially the Grass Group, because you too over the years have shared the agony and ecstasy of cross country running, training and racing. May you all taste success as senior distance runners as well as in whatever career paths you follow. Life is for living- make the most of it.

Thank you parents: that's the long suffering ones, who over the years have turned out to offer support and encouragement to their children, and like them, battled the elements after sometimes travelling far and wide to do so.

Thank you to my growing family: in those early days your support meant more to me than you'll ever know.

And finally, thank you Pam: writing this book for me was easy knowing you'd be doing all the hard work by putting it together.

Foreword

The sport of long-distance running is simple and straightforward; a group of people race each other from a start line to a finish line and there may be anything from five kilometers to 42.2 kilometers between those two lines. It is easy to understand what runners do but not so easy to understand why they do it. It often involves training alone, in the dark and cold, after a hard day's work. Racing always involves pushing oneself to the point of pain with no guarantee of success. Cross country running adds energy-draining cold, slippery mud to the effort and discomfort.

After more than 20 years as a competitive runner, I still struggle to explain to a non-runner why anybody does it. I simply tell them that I loved it and everybody I knew in the sport loved it too. I was lucky enough to be very successful, so you might think it was easier for me to love it, but the truth is that I loved it before I was successful. It was my love of the sport that kept me going through all the setbacks and disappointments until I fulfilled my potential.

The winners in every sport are always the ones who receive the plaudits and headlines, but they are just the tip of a large pyramid, made up of thousands of people, who make the sport what it is. The author of this book, Peter Hemming, is one of those. Although he did not reach the highest level, he was undoubtedly a good runner. He was one of those true stalwarts of running without whom the sport cannot exist.

In *Cross Country and All That Stuff* he recounts his experiences of a runner's life, with tales of travelling the country to race through the mud and be a counter for his club team. Dealing with the flooded changing rooms, and races with no actual changing rooms, that many runners have endured. This book is a vivid and entertaining account of a runner's life.

There is, however, more to Peter's story. In the years after his own career had ended, he has given his time, knowledge, experience and enthusiasm to many teenage runners at the start of their athletic journey. Coaching groups of young runners requires commitment, patience, tact and a lot of warm clothing as he stands outside on winter evenings. Rather than push them towards instant results, he guides them towards a long and fulfilling career.

He does it all for nothing because he loves the sport, as you will discover in the pages of this book.

Charlie Spedding
2022

INTRODUCTION

Most distance runners at some time in their lives have run cross country, and still do, but it would probably have been during their school years, in those dreaded P.E. lessons on cold wet miserable winter afternoons that they first discovered how wonderful the experience is; they had no choice. If it was the last lesson of the day, they had no shower either.

Then there are those of us who missed out on that experience completely, we didn't get a chance to run at school, having to wait some years before taking it up as senior club runners. We weren't forced into it; we got cold, wet and covered in mud on wet miserable afternoons by choice.

Many top distance runners race on the country as part of their winter conditioning and can occasionally be seen racing for their club at local league meetings, that's as well as competing in top level invitation and championship events at home and abroad.

On the other hand, dedicated club runners will religiously turn out as often as possible in local league and domestic championship competition, and in all weathers. And, let's not forget, many of those who have worked their way to the highest level will usually have started their road to success as junior club runners; once a club runner, always a club runner!

Despite missing out on the school experience, most of those who came to distance running late (maybe from a different sport) have taken the whole thing just as seriously, possibly more so, inwardly challenging themselves by pushing their bodies to the limits of endurance.

Conversely there are the club runners who are happy just to enjoy the social side of being part of an athletics club, but still being competitive; running round, chatting and generally lapping it all up.

Club runners of all ages and at all levels are the bedrock of distance running and, for them, turning up at a cross country meeting is like going to a family gathering where there's room for everyone and where standards don't really matter.

The club runner is generally loyal to one club, only transferring to another for a valid reason. The most common one is moving to another part of the country, or the world.

Although I spent my running days in London I now live in the North East of England, where distance running is a way of life and where legends are born not made. That was back in the halcyon days of athletics. The halcyon days I'm referring to being specifically between the middle and the end of the twentieth century. I was in awe of those legends, some whom became my heroes; my heroes are scattered around all the regions of the United Kingdom. Their feats became the inspiration for my own achievements which were modest in comparison.

Having taken up running relatively late in life it's fair to say I was never going to emulate my heroes by reaching the dizzy heights of the Olympic podium, which is where some of them ended up. So instead of writing about Olympic glory and life at the top, this book is about my experiences as a dedicated club runner, which many other club runners, then and now, will relate to.

I achieved my own level of success through an inner belief and a sheer hard work ethic. There were no short cuts, because short cuts in distance running just don't exist.

When I took it up, the so called 'running boom' hadn't really started, it was embryonic and came shortly after, at a time when athletics, which includes cross country and all that stuff, was still being televised regularly. As an armchair athlete I remember watching and thinking, 'One day I'll run like those guys,' yet not for one moment ever really appreciating the years of hard work and the thousands of miles those guys had put in, many starting as juniors, to reach the top, and a place on that victory podium; any victory podium. My full appreciation came later.

It didn't though, stop my competitive nature taking over, because if that's what it took to get the best out of myself then I was up for the challenge, but it was all down to me and my sheer bloody mindedness, stubborn determination and some natural ability, to achieve success! My interpretation of the word success is: achieving what you set out to achieve! For distance runners it's about having mental strength as well as physical ability, the ratio being around 5% physical - 95% mental. And it's not just about having the will to win; more importantly, it's about applying it. As a competitive runner that was my philosophy and as a coach of junior distance runners (and the occasional senior) it always has been; I'm just passing that philosophy on.

Although I didn't reach anywhere near the same level of success as my heroes, it wasn't for the lack of trying, because just like thousands of other club runners up and down the country, I turned out, summer and winter, competing on the road, the track and cross country, always giving my very best, turning myself inside out for the club as well as for my own personal success.

Distance runners as a breed are usually solitary individuals and to get anywhere near the top of the sport, or even to become an average club runner, have to be single minded, selfish even, but above all else they have to be self motivated, not money motivated with dreams of Premier League glory.

THE FIRST STEPS

As a species we are born to run! Our first steps as toddlers weren't walking steps; we ran (or at least tried to) across the floor from one parent's outstretched arms to the other parent who was sitting on the opposite side of the room. Running is not rocket science. It's a matter of putting one foot in front of the other, it's a kind of magic, and the faster you run the more magical it becomes. It's a great feeling.

Our ancestors, being hunter gatherers were less fortunate than us, they ran hundreds of miles chasing their next meal, and if they didn't catch it they went hungry; that was all the motivation they needed! No roads or motorways. They were the original distance runners......running cross country.

So for us humans, running is the most natural thing in the world. It's in our DNA.

PART 1: 1977/78

As a runner have you ever asked yourself, 'Why did I start running?' Go on ask yourself, and then when you've thought about it answer the question. Then answer this next question, 'Because there are times when it hurts so much that I can't carry on, then why did I?'

For me it all started one evening in October 1977. I was watching television and without warning a sharp stabbing pain shot through my chest causing me to cry out loud; I was smoking a cigarette at the time.

The following morning I saw the doctor, or to be correct, she saw me and checked me over, concentrating on my chest and lungs, while at the same time telling me to breathe deeply; which I did. Then she popped the question, 'Mr. Hemming how many cigarettes do you smoke a day?' Good question, but how did she know I was a smoker, I hadn't said a word. 'About ten,' I lied. In reality it was closer to fifty; that's right, five zero. She continued, 'By the sound of your lungs I guess it's more so I'm advising you to cut it down, or better still give it up completely, because if you don't you could be dead in two years!'

To hide my fear I replied in typical gung ho fashion, 'But doctor I'm too young to die.' I was approaching my 30th birthday. 'I'm serious,' she retorted, 'Come back and see me in two weeks,' and with that she gave me a sick note to cover the time off work.

'Why put off until tomorrow what you can do today?' I thought, strolling home pondering my future without cigarettes. Up until then I'd smoked for about fifteen years but I haven't touched one since that morning at the doctors. It was a lesson in how to give up smoking; the quick way.

As soon as I got home I bit the bullet, slipped on an old, beat up tennis track suit (which really wasn't suitable for running) and a pair of green flash tennis shoes (they weren't ideal either) and went for a run in Ravenor Park, which, conveniently was just round the corner from home. Now this is where the memory fades a little, did I run one or two laps of the park? Whichever, it doesn't really matter because by the time I got back indoors I felt as though death was imminent, never mind in two years. 'If the smoking doesn't get me the running will,' were my thoughts as I lay prostrate on the sofa, sweating buckets and wondering if I'd ever make it to the bathroom; that's how bad it was. I didn't realise how wonderful a shower could be; exhilarating and reviving describes it perfectly considering the circumstances.

In the meantime I went cold turkey and gave up smoking forever, while at the same time beginning to run seriously; oh yes; it really was serious, a serious wake up call. Over the years I'd played football and tennis and considered myself to be reasonably fit; on that day I realised just how fit I really was, or more to the point, how fit I wasn't! I was in terrible shape. I was, though, inspired! In the early 1970's I served in the Royal Air Force, where I played football and tennis to a reasonable standard, and was matey with a guy called Roger. He'd packed in smoking and taken up running, but not only that, he was rubbing shoulders with some of the country's top distance runners who were also servicemen. So I thought, if he can do it, then so can I; so I did.

I was living in West London at the time and after a few months of what I considered training, was in decent shape; but it didn't take long to realise I was kidding myself and would have to work much harder to become the best, or at least to achieve some sort of success.

I never did become the best, at least not on the big stage of distance running, but time and again I pushed myself through the pain barrier to the limits of endurance in an attempt to achieve my own version of success; at that point I wasn't really sure what success meant in running terms! But I'd find out soon enough.

The next step was to put together some sort of plan, something very basic.

THE PLAN

Now that I knew where my running future lay, the logical thing was to join a running club, but that wouldn't be for a while, at least until I was running fit and in better shape, and because I was dedicated and enthusiastic that wouldn't take long; at least that's what I thought!

The Plan therefore, was to give myself a year in which to develop stamina, strength and speed. The other thing I needed of course, was to build up confidence, because the last thing I wanted was to be intimidated or humiliated by other more experienced club runners. But I didn't need to worry because I soon found that runners, especially distance runners, are the least intimidating or humiliating people around; friendly, yes; intimidating and humiliating, definitely not. It was also at about that time that I'd ditched the green flash and bought a pair of proper training shoes.

After I'd been running for about six months I got A SCARE! Habitual smokers who have been at it for years develop a chesty cough (or worse), especially first thing in the morning as they head to the bathroom to cough up and deposit the 'rubbish' that has collected in their lungs from the day before. That's what happened to me, except mine was disgustingly black. Needless to say, I was frightened and it meant another visit to the doctor. She calmed me down, explaining that the 'rubbish' was caused by years of smoking and was now detaching itself from my lungs. 'It's nothing to worry about,' she reassured me, and gave me another sick note. Over the next few weeks my lungs went through a rapid self cleaning process and I carried on running as if nothing had ever happened.

EALING & SOUTHALL ATHLETIC CLUB

I joined Ealing and Southall Athletic Club (now Ealing, Southall and Middlesex Athletic Club.) in October 1978, running my first ever cross country race later that month. By then I was addicted to running, just as I had been to cigarettes for all those years. November and December were hit and miss due to the general aches, pains and tightness in my calf muscles, caused by over training. I was committing the cardinal sin by trying to do too much, too soon. That first year of serious running had been challenging, interesting but above all, enjoyable; there was no turning back.

There would though, be many more challenges and much more enjoyment in the years ahead.

1979 A BAPTISM BY FIRE

The winter of 1978/79 was my first full cross country season. Leading up to Christmas I'd ran in inter-club and league races. It was however, in early January that I got my first experience of racing at a higher level, that was in the Middlesex County Championships at Cockfosters over 7.5 miles. With snow on the ground I ran all of twenty miles that week; including the Middlesex, which I ran in training flats! I received a lot of expert advice that day, much of it to do with the advantages of wearing spikes for running cross country. Because of the tight calf muscles I wasn't sure about spikes, owing to the lack of support they offered (compared to training shoes), but I decided to check some out and made my way, for the first time, to the Sweat Shop in Teddington.

The Sweat Shop was a dedicated shop for runners, run by runners: the Tuck twins, Graham and Grenville, and what they didn't know about running, especially cross country running, wasn't worth knowing. They gave me all the reasons why I should wear spikes but I still wasn't sure and instead left there with a pair of multi studded trainers to run my next big race in: The National Cross Country Championships at Luton. Being the climax of the cross country season I saw it as a chance to break through and make a name for myself in the club, but no-one had warned me that it would be a slog for nine long miles. I was so naïve. It was brutal, but significantly it also meant that making a name for myself would have to wait as I placed 1420th from 1556 finishers. Then, adding insult to my acute embarrassment, I'd run wearing Pete Chiver's number. Officially I hadn't been entered so my name didn't appear in the results, but his did. Pete was a classy runner and was as surprised as anyone, to see his name in the results, and so far down, especially as he hadn't run; but he was well aware of what had happened. I'd been drafted in that day to make up the numbers, but I did make the scoring six in our team result (or at least Pete Chiver's name did). I don't know who was the more embarrassed, him or me; but we laughed about it after. For me though it was a real baptism by fire. That day I vowed never to finish so far back in the National again, I also made sure that in subsequent Nationals I'd be wearing my own number.......and spikes.

The winner that day was Mike McLeod, affectionately known in the running fraternity as the 'Elswick Express,' with Gateshead Harriers taking the team prize to complete the North East double. Mike was a great runner, winning silver in the 10,000 meters at the 1984 Los Angeles Olympics. Whether on the track, the road or cross country, he was feared because of his devastating finishing kick. Now here's the paradox: Elswick Harriers, Mike's club, were a reasonably sized club, yet despite Mike's win finished 58th team, whereas Gateshead who were massive in comparison, packed six in the first sixty. One hundred and seventy teams finished: Ealing were 118th.

In those days The National was run over nine miles, and just like that day at the doctor's surgery, for me it turned out to be a serious wake up call, but I was as enthusiastic as ever and determined to improve. All I had to do was train consistently and avoid injury; yes, that was all!

The year went more or less to plan regarding training, and once the clocks changed I took full advantage of the light evenings to run off road as often as possible, and being 'self coached,' training was based on experimenting with quality, quantity, discipline, determination and pain management.

I quickly found the logistics of training to be straightforward and uncomplicated. There are no courts (or track) to book as in tennis, squash or other court based games; and no-one else needed to be involved as they do when training for team sports. All runners have to do is get their kit on, slip out the door and run, in all weathers, night or day and all year round; it's that easy.

Distance running is a discipline sport, therefore it's down to the individual as to how high they've set their bar and how much success they want; success in distance running isn't served up on a plate.

FELL RUNNING

One of the many advantages of living in West London was that there was plenty of opportunity to run on open green spaces which were ideal for training; fields, parks, golf courses and miles of towpath along the Grand Union Canal, as well as well lit roads, and they were all close to home. I was spoilt for choice and was never bored, as I regularly varied my training routes, on and off road.

I was also varying competition by racing on different surfaces, and although not as prolific as I would later become, I was enjoying everything I did.

Because I very rarely trained on the track it didn't mean I was averse to it. Competing in Open graded, and Southern League track meetings became routine during the spring and summer months, by which time I'd bought a pair of spikes that also doubled up for cross country; specialist cross country spikes were a rarity at the time and only just hitting the shelves in specialist running shops.

In September I recorded 57:27 in my first ten mile road race at Reading, breaking the hour was my goal. Then to really mix things up, in mid October I ran The Worcestershire Beacon Class C mixed surface Fell race in Great Malvern. It started on the road close to the Winter Gardens, before the field left it to climb the well trodden paths to the the highest point of the Malvern Hills, The Worcestershire Beacon itself, which was four hundred and twenty meters above sea level. Once over the top it was a fast and furious descent to finish back at the start.

Fell races were categorised: A, B and C. A: being extremely difficult. B: very difficult and C: just difficult. Despite the thrill of running flat out downhill I would never take up fell running more than once a year! It was the climb that got me, the hands-on quadriceps shuffle, and whereas Category C supposedly was just difficult, to me it felt extremely difficult.

Having been brought up in Worcestershire, running The Beacon was an opportunity to spend the weekend with my parents who still lived in the county, near Evesham. It was also a change to run in the beauty of the lush green Worcestershire countryside. Travelling far and wide to races became a regular occurrence, adding variety to the pleasures of running.

The various race venues, on and off road, was what made running so interesting, especially when comparing some of the Metropolitan League cross country courses that were located in and around the Greater London area. For example, the narrow tracks and steep climbs in Ruislip woods, or the severe undulations and mud of Parliament Hill Fields to the pancake flat Cranford Park and the wide open space of Wormwood Scrubs common. There was no comparison. But the reality was, the flatter the course the better I liked it and ran some of my better races on those flatter courses! And because I was wearing spikes I was able to keep upright in the muddiest of terrains and conditions.

It was the same with road racing. Courses up and down the country varied widely and runners travelled far and wide to compete, often incorporating a race as part of a weekend break!

One such weekend for me was spent in the beautiful Cotswold village of Bourton on the Water where I raced 15 miles over a two lap course which included a torturous climb up the notorious Rissington Hill (which is hard enough to drive up). But what I wasn't prepared for was the effect that two helpings of apple and blackcurrant crumble from the night before would have on me, or to be precise, my stomach, which forced two pit stops in the last two miles. And although not being too happy at having to stop, I was quite pleased to finish inside ninety minutes, just; 1:29:53. Although stopping cost me dearly I learnt a lesson that weekend...... be careful what you eat, and how much, the night before a race.

It wasn't only the variety of venues that made life interesting, because as I quickly learnt, on my travels, runners by and large are friendly and always up for a chat. They were then and still are, so to start a conversation with a total stranger was as natural as going for a run.

The year had been a massive learning curve as I found just how far the body could be, and could not be pushed. My first serious injury, the achilles tendon, forced complete rest during four weeks, spanning April and May. Recovery is important and should be a key word in the distance runner's dictionary and mind.

1980 MILESTONES

January 1st 1980 not only heralded in a new decade, but on a personal level there were three major milestones during the year; the most momentous was the birth of my daughter, Clare, I started a new job and I entered my first marathon. It was also the year I trained seriously on the track!

During the winter, Ealing and Southall competed in the Metropolitan Cross Country League against various other clubs from the greater London area, but as well as the Met. League there were annual championship events: The Greater London Council (GLC.) North of the Thames, The Middlesex County, The Southern area and The National,

My run in the Middlesex in early January was a disaster, having failed to make the scoring six for the team competition. I was obviously disappointed, which only made me more determined to make amends in The Southern four weeks later. That day however, started much earlier then expected as the warning signs that the birth of a baby was imminent. Those signs started just before the dawn on February 9th, It was later that morning at 11.53 that I helped to deliver Clare, in Perivale Maternity Hospital. Now when I say helped to deliver, what I really mean is I was there doing my best to avoid getting in the way and trying to keep as calm as possible through it all.

Needless to say, after such an eventful and emotional morning the race was a bit of an anti-climax; as my training diary reads: 'What a race, I had to be lowered from the clouds to get to the starting line. I drifted round in a nonchalant relaxed manner, the mud was deep and I felt good, a good last lap.' I didn't usually drift round three laps of Parliament Hill, but on that afternoon I did, and I wasn't particularly bothered whether I made the scoring six or not.

I don't recall much of the week between The Southern and the Hillingdon 5 mile road race the following Saturday. After collecting Mother and daughter from the hospital I got a pass out and drove to Ruislip for my first run in the ultra fast 5 for the first time; recording 27:25.

All good things come to an end, and sadly, the last running of that 'Classic' race was in 2004.

SERIOUS TRACK TRAINING

When I first joined the club I trained on the track at Spike's Bridge, but at the time I wasn't really sure why or what good it was doing me, so not being the sort of person to dismiss something out of hand I thought I'd give it another go. It was July when Les Smith and I decided to sharpen up and do some serious track training. We met each week and ran on the cinder track at Drayton Green, Ealing. Now this track was laid in 1928 and it was 352 meters to the lap with not a lane marking in sight; there was no doubt, it had seen better days. We did 5 weekly sessions and for whatever the reason called it a day after the fifth one. I'm not sure if either of us benefitted from those sessions; but for me it was very boring. I got more enjoyment from the twenty minute run to the track and the twenty minute warm down, running home.

TAYLOR WOODROW ATHLETIC CLUB
THE NEW JOB

I started in mid March in my new role as the brickwork instructor at Taylor Woodrow, the International Construction and Civil Engineering Company, (now Taylor Wimpey, the house builder) at their head office training centre, which, conveniently was only a short walk from home.

Not long after starting there I was contacted by an 'unknown' colleague, Laurie Kelly. Laurie was involved with The London Business Houses Athletic Association and invited me to work with him to form the Taylor Woodrow Athletic Club; which I did. He took responsibility for much of the admin. duties, whereas I filled the role of team captain, and Trevor Jones, who worked in the publicity department, dealt with all things involving publicity; naturally. There was no formal committee, it ran like clockwork without one.

The company was very supportive, and Dick Puttick, the Taylor Woodrow Group Chairman accepted our invitation and became the club president. What a team!

A few days after the initial meeting with Laurie, I turned up at the Ealing and Southall AGM and left the meeting finding myself on the committee as Press Secretary; how did that happen!

Fitting running round my family life became a well worked routine, although at times it seemed it was taking over completely. I was though, given every support and things just fell into place; life then, couldn't have been sweeter.

MARATHON DEBUT

With less than two years serious running experience I felt confident enough to run a marathon and entered the Rugby event, which took place in early September. As a small family unit we took every opportunity to get away at weekends and the trip to Rugby was a chance for Clare to see her grand parents, and for them to see her, so we broke the journey and stayed overnight en-route to the race.

After a solid eight week build up of consistent training Rugby wasn't quite the debut I'd hoped for, and worse. It was very hot! Being a bricklayer I knew a thing or two about walls, but I wasn't prepared for the one I hit just before twenty miles. It meant dragging myself up 'Carthorse Hill', a 1-in-7 gradient, for a third and final time, managing to complete the last six miles in just over the hour to finally clock 3:32:27. Come what may I was determined to finish, as my training diary reads: 'It would've taken a landslide to have stopped me.'

Having done the distance at Rugby I knew what to expect in the next marathon I did, and 'Carthorse Hill' wouldn't feature in it. I was disappointed, and just as after the Luton National I swore to never run a marathon that slow again. The surprising thing however, was that Rugby didn't take as much out of me as I thought it would, but then running it that slowly I can understand why.

Here are some brief statistics which I'm sure will enlighten the reader, marathon runner or not, as to just how severe the course was: John Bigham, the winner, ran 2:26:23 and was the only competitor to break 2:30:00. Of the 117 finishers only 34 ran under 3 hours. There were 8 DNF.

Despite my disappointment, and because of the pre-race training I was strong and recovered enough to run the Reading 10 two weeks later in a PB time of 56.07 (1979: 57.27)

After Reading, everything was going smoothly so three weeks later I returned to Malvern to run the Worcestershire Beacon again. Ever heard of a runner forgetting his racing shoes? It happens, but thankfully I borrowed a pair of Adidas TRX trainers off Paul Haywood, the proprietor of a running shop in Worcester. I ran hard, getting a PB. there, as well as blistered toes from shoes my feet weren't used to, but annoyingly I also picked up a knee injury attempting to clear a ditch on the fast descent to the finish, but because it was only a 'niggle' of an injury, I was convinced that I would be able to run through it, and I did, on and off. But it flared up and I was restricted to training every other day over short distances, but in the end I had to stop. Fortunately, and soon after, I met senior coach and life long Ealing club member Ron Jewkes, who like me was spectating at the Met.

League at Ruislip, and because I wasn't running he wanted to know why, so I told him. He gave me some strengthening exercises to do and within a couple of weeks I was running again. Over the Christmas period, starting on Christmas Day, I ran four short road races back to back and thankfully the knee held up.

1981 IT'S ALL ABOUT WINNING

Happy New Year, I wish. Do runners ever learn, and in particular this one!!! After the four Christmas races, I then competed every weekend throughout January and suffered the consequences with a recurrence of the knee injury. I was though, fortunate to get an immediate appointment at the Athletes clinic at Hillingdon Hospital. Then after two weeks of complete rest, some intense physio sessions and exercising at home, I quickly returned to fitness. In early March, my saviour, Doctor Peter Sperryn, gave me the all clear to run, so I did. I was fortunate to get away with my impatience, inexperience and stupidity so lightly!

JULIAN GOATER AND 'THAT' NATIONAL!

The National was held at Parliament Hill, and because I was still nursing the knee, I went along to spectate and give my club mates a shout, and what a decision that turned out to be; because what I witnessed that Saturday afternoon was an awesome, unforgettable display of front running by the Shaftesbury Harrier Julian Goater. He led from gun to tape, leaving the cream of British distance runners in his wake, winning by almost two minutes, a margin that has never been equalled, and is never likely to be, at least not over nine miles. Since 1998 The National has been run over the shorter distance of approximately 12 km whereas, at the time, nine miles was the standard distance.

Although winning the individual title was a massive achievement, there was also the hotly contested team championship which that day was won by the Midlands club, Tipton Harriers.

The National was also the qualifying race for the World Cross Country Championship, held a few weeks later in Madrid, with the first nine finishers at Parliament Hill being selected to run for England! Julian Goater finished 4th in Madrid, therefore missing out on the bronze medal by four seconds; being Spain it's possible there wasn't enough mud for his liking, unlike Parliament Hill! England were 6th team. Needless to say, with so much at stake The National was the biggest domestic cross country race on the calendar, not only in terms of the number of competitors, but also in status. Year after year the who's who of the country's top distance runners turned up to compete against us lesser mortals. In how many other sports would that mix be possible!

For most club runners, to run nine miles at Parliament Hill was a feat of mind numbing endurance, and as if that wasn't punishment enough, anyone wanting a decent shower had no chance. But those that did and were brave enough could, but it meant washing in tin baths full of cold muddy water before going home. So imagine then being a Gateshead Harrier, (who that day were runners up in the team race) you would have had to fight for a place in one of those tin baths to get as clean as possible before heading to King's Cross for the three hour train journey back to Newcastle and other destinations in the north east. The alternative was to forego the bath and cringe as the mud dried and tugged at the hair on tired legs.

Knowing I would never run the way Julian Goater did that day I was, nonetheless inspired and in my own way would go on to inspire and motivate others in due course.

Although enjoying the natural freedom of running on the country I couldn't skate across the mud the way some runners could, but for me cross country running served an important purpose, it was an excellent way of developing strength, which it did. After a winter of racing and training on hills and through ankle deep mud I was always strong, so to compliment that strength and to improve speed I ran regular fartlek sessions off road; running free and as one with nature, as often as possible.

Five weeks after The National I was back at Parliament Hill to race 3000m on the track, with no mud and not a tin bath in sight. The race turned out to be a battle of wills between club mate Roland Humphries and myself, as we exchanged the lead several times before I finally opened up a winning gap with two laps to go. Winning - that's what competition is about. It was my first ever win and a very special experience, one of a handful that I have cherished over the years.

Had watching the National inspired me to go to the front from so far out? Or was it that I had felt confident enough to win it? Probably both, I can't say, but what I can say is that winning is very special at whatever age and level of competition you're at. Although I made the decision to go for the win early, my message to all athletes, seniors and juniors, is never go to the front unless you know you can win the race, and it doesn't matter whether you've got one lap of a 1500m track race to go; or 15 miles of a marathon left, or even if you're in the home straight with the tape in sight. Ultimately, that's a decision only the runner can make and it takes absolute belief, total commitment and 100% confidence in one's own ability. Having that attitude is what turns good runners into champions. It's a state of mind; if you think you can't you won't, but if you believe you can you will.

COACH OR MENTOR?

Although I was never formally coached, some of the more experienced Ealing distance runners were more than willing to guide and advise me in any way they could, the rest was down to me and how I planned and implemented my own training and racing.

One who was more than happy to help was a long distance specialist, Dave Case. The word mentor is freely used in coaching circles especially where juniors are concerned, and although I wasn't a junior that's what Dave was to me; not a coach as such, but a mentor, a friend who offered guidance freely. He was a one off and a master of pace judgement, and although I didn't always get pace right in the early days, especially in the middle distance races, generally his advice stuck.

So imagine my pride and delight when I finished ahead of him in the Chichester to Portsmouth 25km road race. Although we got on really well Dave had always been on my hit list of club mates to beat! After the race, as well as offering his congratulations, he gave me a sound piece of advice that I've never forgotten, 'Pete, whatever you're doing in training don't change it, because it's working.' What he said was, 'if it ain't broke, don't fix it'. There will of course always be exceptions to those words of wisdom. A mix of quality and quantity was what my training was based on.

Distance running isn't rocket science. It never has been and never will be, and yet training methods, diet, as well as science and technology have affected and benefited many in the modern sport. Athletes, whether sprinters or marathon runners, build their training on a foundation of stamina and strength. Get those two right then everything else will fall into place with the correct training; and that doesn't happen overnight. Perfecting training really is a marathon not a sprint. Excuse the pun!

THE DIET

With the ghost of the Rugby Marathon hanging over me like a dark cloud I entered the Polytechnic Marathon (The Poly) as a way of proving to myself that Rugby was a one off! The Poly, held in June, was unique insomuch that it started in the grounds of Windsor Castle and followed the Long Walk before turning right at the Copper Horse Statue of King George III (that's third not one hundred and eleven) to continue mainly on the roads around Windsor Great Park, before finishing back in the town, on the track at Vansittart Road, which, since Millennium year has no longer been there. It's been relocated, and replaced by an all weather eight lane track on the other side of the town near Eton college, close to the confluence of the Jubilee River and the River Thames. The last running of the Poly was in 1996. And just like the Hillingdon 5, it is another great race that has been consigned to the annals of athletic history.

Unlike Rugby, as part of my marathon preparation I tried 'The Diet' or at least my version of it! Basically, 'The Diet' means cutting out all carbohydrate foods, starting a week before the race, then with two days to go, excluding race day, the 'carbo loading' phase begins. During the loading phase (which really is a two day eating binge) the excess carbohydrate intake is stored in the muscles to provide enough fuel, therefore avoiding glycogen depletion in the latter stages of the race. That supposedly, prevents the runner from hitting the dreaded wall; at least that's how it's supposed to work.

Because I'd never done 'The Diet' before, my version consisted of reducing carbohydrates, although not completely; but it didn't matter anyway, because as I was about to start the loading phase an attack of gastro-enteritis hit me. My two loading days were spent either in bed or in the bathroom, which meant no marathon for me. 'Was the diet to blame for my sickness?' I'll never know, but whereas Dave's 'if it ain't broke don't fix it' advice normally held me in good stead, then my own would too, because when it comes to diet if it's balanced and works then don't tamper with it; and remember, what works for one doesn't always work for others. Getting it right is a matter of trial and error from day one; that's day one of becoming a distance runner.

I put the disappointment of not running The Poly behind me and got on with normal life, then once back in to my regular eating habits it didn't take long to fully recover and resume a summer of consistent training and racing, on the track and the road, and for a change, over shorter distances.

Part of that normal life involved working for a living, which I enjoyed almost as much as running and Taylor Woodrow had turned out to be a good employer, whose philosophy, like my own, was a belief in training and development. That much so that in mid September they sent me on a five day Team Leadership course to Cornelyn Manor in Anglesey. The course involved a variety of physically testing outdoor pursuits; including rock climbing, orienteering, kayaking and mountain walking. The delegates had been split into four four-man groups with one being assigned the role of team leader each day, by the course instructors. I led the team for the mountain walking. As the team leader I was responsible for the group and made all the decisions; the instructors only intervened if those decisions risked any danger to life or limb.

When all the activities had finished for the day it was well into the evening and time for dinner, which was followed by the brief and preparation for the following day's activity. Bearing that in mind I decided to train in the early morning before breakfast; it was either that or not run at all.

Cornelyn Manor overlooked the Menai Straits with the mountains of Snowdonia forming the backdrop, like a Constable landscape; how could I not run with a view like that to look forward to every morning. It was a loop of just over 3 miles, descending for the first half with a steep climb to finish. Those morning runs set me up for the day; whereas the other guys thought I was totally mad.

Mad or not, I learnt a lot about myself over those five days as well as the three core needs of training! Imagine there are three equal sized circles. They represent the three training needs that teamwork is based on; they are: the needs of the task, of the team and of the individual. Now link them together (like the Olympic rings) The linking of those rings signifies that each need is as important as the other.

All too soon summer was gone which meant it was time to screw the long pins in to the spikes for the cross country season which, as usual, started in early October at The Horsenden Relays.

CROSS COUNTRY RUNNING - THE CAMARADERIE

As a rule, distance runners are single minded and goal focused, and if they're not they should be! That single mindedness is dictated by the nature of the sport, because if the athlete isn't prepared to train, no-one can, or will, make them. Whatever the time of day, whether it's as the sun is on the rise or the dead of night, or if the temperature is below freezing or hotter than hell, it doesn't matter; the dedicated athlete will always find the time and the place to run; whether at home or away; away in this instance can mean anywhere: on holiday; on business; it doesn't matter where.

It's also to do with time management, which is why it's essential to keep a training diary; a journal that is not just to record what you've done, but equally as important, to plan ahead and to organise what you're going to do.

As well as being dedicated individuals, there is a camaraderie between distance runners which manifests itself particularly in the cross country season, when, especially at inter-club and league matches, all club members get a chance to run. It doesn't matter what their standard is, or the standard they think they are, because that's when the team effort really counts; it's also when the fun starts (not that it doesn't in the championship events). It's at those inter-club and league races when club mates became rivals, forcing the best out of each other as they battle to become scorers for the team. It was early in the cross country season when I caught up with some of the lads from other clubs, as well as with my own club mates, who I hadn't seen all summer. It was really a general catch up; a time for exchanging results and reflecting on what had happened since the previous cross country season.

By the winter of 1981 running had become a big part of my life and I trained at least once a day, everyday, wherever I was and whenever I could, even on holiday. For the serious club runner there should always be a bona fide reason for not training, but as always there can and will be exceptions, but those exceptions should always be valid and never become a pathetic excuse.

Despite the drop in mileage, over the year I had raced prolifically and was reasonably pleased with the results, yet I was aware that I was nowhere close to achieving my true potential. I knew there was more fuel in the tank, it just meant tapping it. As the year end approached, as always, I looked forward to Christmas Day morning and the gift race at Ruislip!

1982 ANOTHER MARATHON BUT NO DIET!

I couldn't have wished for a better start to the new year having trained consistently and injury free, racing virtually every weekend right up to The National in March.

At the beginning of January there was though a rare occurrence, something almost unheard of in cross country lore. It concerned the Met. League fixture at Woodford. Mike phoned to say it had been cancelled: CROSS COUNTRY CANCELLED; whatever next. The officials had been out to inspect the course, but because of deep snow drifts they couldn't find it. The cancellation of a cross country meeting due to inclement weather was almost unheard of, at least as far as I can remember.

I'd had a full winter of training and competition and as always there was real strength in my legs and mental toughness in my head! Just two weeks after a decent run in The National at Roundhay Park, Leeds, (at least by my standards) I was on the road again, travelling to Bath to run my first half marathon, where, and importantly I'd be putting Dave's advice regarding pace judgement to the test. In truth, and despite the Chichester-Portsmouth run I was still on a steep learning curve.

I was in reasonable shape having ran a PB of 26.14 in the Hillingdon 5 course two weeks before The National and felt confident, knowing Bath was a flat two lap course; ideal for a fast time then?

The start was in the city centre and followed an out and back course along the river basin, before heading back to finish in the city centre. Being flat didn't make it any easier or less painful; just faster. Pain is the same whether it's flat or hilly, which means the faster you run the less time you spend hurting! I felt great, finishing 44th in a huge field, clocking 71.46. My thoughts after the race were 'This is a distance I really enjoy running.' Yet despite the pounding and unyielding surface of the road it was road racing that I really enjoyed, more than the track, and yes, even more than cross country. Actually, and truthfully, I just loved running on any surface, it didn't really matter which.

In late April, four weeks after Bath, I ran The Finchley 20 which was four laps of the 'slightly undulating' Hillingdon 5. However, by the time I'd got to the fourth lap those slight undulations felt more like steep hills. That day The Finchley celebrated its 50th anniversary and incorporated the prestigious Inter-Counties, and Southern Counties Championships.

Within those four weeks between Bath and The Finchley I'd ran The Thames Valley Harriers (TVH.) Road Relays at Cranford, The Southern 12 Stage Road Relays, then held at Wimbledon common, The Maidenhead 10 and just four days before the Finchley, 3000m on the track at High Wycombe; running Personal Bests in every one.

The Finchley turned out to be a real Ealing and Southall team effort as Rob Howells, Chris Canton and myself picked up medals for the winning team in the Middlesex Championship race. It was a great day and what a fantastic feeling. Records and times can be beaten and bettered but no-one can take a medal away, it's yours forever. The icing on the cake was that I ran a PB of 1:57:00. that day.

So having run reasonable times over the half marathon, 10 and 20 miles, I decided to have another crack at the marathon, choosing to travel away again, that time to Gloucester.

The race was held in early October which I approached with an eight week build up, tapering back over the final two, but not daring to risk 'The Diet' again. Over those eight weeks I ran an average of 70 miles a week, the highest; 86.5, the lowest 41. Physically I was ready, but also a bit nervous, because, as everyone who has ever ran a marathon knows, anything can happen on the day no matter how well the preparation has gone, or how good you're feeling, which of course I'd found out to my cost at Rugby. But it wasn't Rugby and I was mentally up for it; totally focused and relaxed.

The weather at Gloucester was ideal for the 10.30 start in the city centre park. The course then zig-zagged through the inner city streets, mainly for the benefit of the spectators lining them, and who were very supportive. The course then headed out in to the country on mainly flat roads, (a bridge across a dual carriageway was the only gradient to speak of) before heading back to the city, finishing in the same park where the race had started. Stopping my watch on the finish line I glanced at it and smiled.

Thankfully the changing rooms were only a short walk from the finish so I decided to have a quick shower so as not to spend the journey home smelling the way runners do after spending over two and a half hours on the road.

Quick shower; not quite? sitting in that changing room was the first time I'd ever suffered post race cramps, severe cramps, in both calf muscles. Sitting and standing was fine, it was leaning forward to unlace my shoes that the pain really got me. For a while, reaching those laces was impossible, and the more I tried the worse the pain got; and what's more, I was on my own, there was no-one I could call on for help. I did actually think about showering with the shoes on but eventually managed to get them off and the hot water worked wonders at soothing the cramps.

Once again I marvelled at just how exhilarating a shower was, oh the simple pleasures of life! Despite the long journey back to London, I didn't cramp up on the drive. There was no smell either!

And the result: I was sandwiched between club mates Rob and Rod to finish19th in 2:36:05 from 1352 finishers. I'd smashed my PB. by running almost an hour faster than at Rugby. To say I was pleased was an understatement even though getting under 2:30:00. would have been a real bonus. And although I was a very happy man that day, there was one man who wasn't!

The Horsenden Relays and The Gloucester clashed: same weekend different day. Missing the relays invariably meant incurring the wrath of cross country captain Mike Barratt, but so as to appease him I promised to be available for the rest of the cross country season. However, it wasn't so much that I'd gone AWOL on my own, so too had key runners Rob and Rod, who would certainly have made the relay 'A' team; nevertheless I still got the flak for their and my absence.

Getting an ear bashing from Mike was par for the course; that was his way, he spoke his mind, got it off his chest, then forgot it. He was a major driving force in the club and a real inspiration to me because of his dedication and enthusiasm. If it wasn't for people like Mike (known in the running fraternity as 'Evergreen') athletics in this country, certainly at club level would die. There's a Mike Barratt in every athletic club up and down the country, and it doesn't matter whether they're active runners, committee members, team captains or whatever, or in Mike's case, just a driving force.

Despite pledging my support for the cross country season; Gloucester wasn't my last road race of the year. There was one I'd ran for the first time in 1980 and which I'd looked forward to running every year since. It was a road race hosted by Hillingdon Athletic Club on Christmas Day morning: the 3.2 mile 'Gift Race' and although low key it was highly competitive; and the gift? Competitors were invited to take a gift, which was usually bottle shaped, and place it on the large table in the middle of the club house, along with other wrapped goodies! The race winner took first pick of the gifts, second choice to the runner up and so on. However, runners not taking a gift, couldn't claim one. That race was an ideal way of working up an appetite and getting in to the Christmas spirit(s.)

Training through the year had gone well with only a handful of days lost, mainly due to moving house in May, and the subsequent work that entailed; re-wiring, decorating and much more DIY.

1983 MONDAY NIGHTS WILL NEVER BE THE SAME AGAIN!

Although 1982 had been a great year 1983 saw two major events, the biggest being a family affair; the birth of Thomas in November, and in the Spring the club took up residency in the club house of Pitshanger Dynamo Football Club for Monday evenings training.

I don't know who instigated the move, the committee I suppose, and although I was on it, it came as news to me; good news. Having a base, just for one evening a week, was like a breath of fresh air being blown in to the club as there were so many benefits, the most important one being that we had a place to meet, train and socialise. It was a positive step forwards, a quantum leap towards team building, which I knew something about having done the course!

Being the headquarters of a football club the facilities were everything we could've wished for; spacious changing rooms with adequate showers, and in the club house itself there was a dart board, pool table and space for our own notice board, but crucially there was a well stocked bar, and as all distance runners know, where there's a bar and a congregation there's always going to be serious banter, and there was - every Monday. That banter however, and the socialising that went with it had to wait until later in the evening after some very serious training had taken place.

There were various groups of all ages and abilities; male and female, from juniors to battle scarred distance runners; seniors and veterans. Being a Monday, some, mostly the battle scarred distance runners had probably done a long run the day before, so the intention on Mondays was to take it easy, (the key word being 'intention') and treat it as a social recovery run! The reality though was very different. The recovery lasted about 10 minutes which was about as long as it took for the muscles to start warming; that then was the signal to gradually increase the tempo to a more serious competitive pace with the finish always ending in a burn up; and the recovery run? I'm not sure if there ever was one, except perhaps during those first ten minutes. And the social? That took place in the bar over the banter and a well earned pint, or conversely a pint over well earned banter!

A couple of weeks after the move to the club house, at the club's half yearly meeting, I found myself appointed Vice cross country captain, therefore adding to my existing Press Secretary role and working closely with Mike Barratt which turned out to be an interesting two man collaboration and a real eye opener. At the same meeting the club officially went from male only to 'unisex.'

The Ladies section of the club was born and almost immediately new members joined in their droves. I had passed on all the information to the Sports Editor at The Ealing Gazette weekly newspaper who gave both events, the club house and going 'unisex', excellent headline coverage.

As well as the Gazette publicity, the club did their own. Bright yellow A4 posters were printed and displayed in appropriate locations around the borough. Those flyers were an excellent way of increasing membership, which is exactly what happened. Then, in addition to the existing publicity, Rob Howells, our in-house graphic designer/editor, launched the quarterly club magazine, Ealing Athletics, which consisted of pages filled with interesting club information.

I always regarded myself as being a one club man and I was, so when the Monday move to the club house took place there was no-one happier than me. Those Hillingdon Christmas morning Gift Races were an insight to what an athletics club is like when it has an established base, not just a track, or a pub with a back or upstairs room. Clubs need a social base as well as a functional meeting place. The very first time I went there I thought 'Wow, this is an amazing set up, why doesn't our club have something similar?' Hillingdon were a successful club and hosted two iconic road races, and with the Ruislip woods on the door step, they had a great ready made cross country venue too. I was tempted at one time to transfer over, but, like I said I was a one club man and Monday nights were never the same again and I always looked forward to them.

At about the same time as the clubhouse move, members of Taylor Woodrow Athletic Club were invited to a London Marathon publicity gathering at St. Katherine's Dock which proved to be invaluable for those wanting to run the marathon, but who didn't have the qualifying time! There was an agreement that they could enter by by-passing the ballot system.

In the meantime my own running continued as normal; well almost. The plan, yes another one, was to reduce mileage and focus more on developing speed, by running fartlek and other speed based sessions; but which didn't involve running on the track. Despite not training on the track, what I had in mind was to race on it during the summer, especially over 3000 and 5000m.

During the track and field season Ealing and Southall competed in the Southern league where I was usually selected to run the 5000m, the distance that suited me most and crucially the one I was best at. Clubs could enter two athletes, an 'A' and 'B' string, in all events...... track and field. On the track, the 'A' string runner was always expected to finish ahead of the 'B' string runner; however it wasn't always the case.

There was one time when Mike was short of steeplechase runners and tried convincing me that it was my event, saying it would be good experience, which rang a familiar bell, all the way back to Luton and that first National; I said I'd think about it. After closely inspecting the barriers, especially the water jump, I said 'No thank you.' He got the message and didn't ask again, and I never offered and carried on running the 5000m. Southern League meetings usually ran to a strict timetable and because relegation and promotion was at stake, competition was fierce, fierce enough for top flight internationals to be drafted in to compete for their clubs.

Unlike the Met. League, the Southern League covered a much wider geographical area with venues not only around London and the south east, but as far afield as the west country.

On the other hand, 'Open' graded track meetings were closer to home, the closest being a ten minute drive to West London Stadium (re-named The Linford Christie Stadium) in East Acton, or, the furthest I ever travelled was a twenty five minute drive in the opposite direction along the A40 to the track at Handycross, High Wycombe, which, like the Vansittart Road track at Windsor has since re-located.

Those graded meetings were very popular and for me served as the ultimate in training for speed. They too were scheduled to run to a timetable, but all too often it went down the pan as more races (usually sprints) were added to meet the demands of those runners entering on the day, or evening, and meant that longer distance races, usually the 3000m or 5000m, which were always the last event of the meeting, could be seriously delayed, in some instances for up to an hour, or even longer. It goes without saying then, that those delays played havoc with the timetable and more annoyingly, with the distance runners' warm up.

The way the grading worked was simple. Athletes were selected to run in a particular race (if there was more than one) according to the times they had declared on their entry forms; Power of 10 didn't exist then. It was a good system and meant runners of similar abilities ran against each other making for good racing: that was the logic behind grading and as a rule it generally worked.

And that big day! The highlight of the year took place at 12.25 on November 29th at Perivale maternity hospital, which was when my son Thomas was born. Once again I was there, doing my best to keep out of the way; which I did. I collected him and his mother four days later, and unlike the last birth in the family that time it didn't clash with a race, and even if it had, there would have been no way I could have got a pass out for a second time.

1983 had been a great year in my family life and prolific as far as racing was concerned, mostly on the track, yet it was two longer distance road races that I was more than pleased with: The inaugural Evesham Half Marathon in early May, and The Reading 10.

Although I hadn't lived in the Evesham area for many years I was more than familiar with the roads the race followed and knew it would be tough; the masochist in me looked forward to the challenge of the hilly course all the same. I ran 77.17 to finish 18th. Not a spectacular time, but the hills turned out to be far more difficult than I'd remembered, after all, the only time I'd ever been round those roads was by car. The Vale of Evesham is a beautiful part of England and there was some stunning scenery on parts of the course, which after a while I never really noticed, stunning or not; when I was truly focused the only thing I saw was what lay ahead: it's called tunnel vision.

The Reading 10, in September, was one of a series of races that constituted the Ealing and Southall road racing championships. I latched on to Rob and ran with him for as long as I could, but couldn't hang on as he pulled away, and in the process dragged me to a PB of 54.04 (previous 56.14). That though was sweet revenge for him as only a few weeks earlier I'd out kicked him coming off the final bend in a 5000m Southern League race at the Withdean track in Brighton; where, as usual, I'd ran as the 'B' string runner!

As the year end approached, the cross country season was well underway and there was a flurry of races, the first being the final Met. League of the year at Parliament Hill, on the weekend before Christmas. I'd driven to Hampstead with Phil Rolls and his boys, Stephen and Richard. As we started walking the course, approaching the top of the first hill, there was an almighty explosion behind us, 'My God Phil, what was that?'

'It sounds like a bomb,' he replied. Turning to look, the sound of the blast faded and in the distance of that famous London skyline a plume of smoke rose like a mysterious ashen finger, before disappearing into the murk of the grey winter's afternoon sky. To us it was ominous, whereas to Londoners generally it came to be known simply as 'The Harrod's Bombing'.

To round the year off, once again on Christmas Day, I drove the short distance to the Hillingdon club house with my gift wrapped, returning there on New Year's Eve to run the two lap mixed terrain 'Round the Lido' race. Two low key races, but high intensity effort in both.

1984 A DISAPPOINTING PERSONAL BEST

Taylor Woodrow, as well as being a major construction and civil engineering company was also a property developer responsible for much of the major re-development around the St. Katherine's Dock area which at the time was part of the London Marathon course. It was immediately after passing through St. Katherine's Dock that all runners were confronted by the infamous cobbled section.

All members of the Taylor Woodrow Athletic Club, because of the connection, could enter the marathon without having to risk the uncertainty of the ballot, which for those without the qualifying time of 2.40.00 for senior men, was a perk worth having. It was also useful insomuch that the extra miles that marathon training demanded could be planned well in advance knowing entry was guaranteed.

My own training consisted of a fifteen week build up which included stepping stone races and a two week taper. At the time it was every serious club runner's ambition to break 2:30.00; and because I was serious it was my ambition too, and for those fifteen weeks the race became an obsession as I lived and breathed running that marathon and breaking that elusive sub 2:30:00 barrier. Third time lucky perhaps?

Leading up to Christmas the cross country season had gone relatively well, but the new year got off to the worst possible start; having to drop out of the Middlesex with a hamstring pull. It responded to a week of self treatment, ice, stretching and light training, if walking can be classed as training. Then having recovered from that setback, four days in to the first week of the fifteen week build up I was laid low with a stomach bug. With total rest and complete fasting for a couple of days the bug cleared and the hamstring, which had been niggling through January loosened up in time for the Southern at Parliament Hill in February. Oh what a day!

A group of us had done the usual warm up: a one lap inspection of the course, then having ran the 3 lap, 9 mile race in the usual Parliament Hill quagmire; we repeated the warm up with a one lap warm down; where, at about half way I finally ran out of steam! Thankfully, as was my habit, there was a bag of post race rations back at the Ealing base camp. Looking back it seems like madness; but it's what we all did then: miles, miles and more miles. I skipped the Hillingdon 5 (the first of the stepping stone races) to concentrate on running more miles. By that time I was well in to the fifteen weeks, which meant that as well as the usual evening runs I was training early mornings too; and just as at Cornelyn Manor, those early runs were a great way to start the day.

I was in the best shape I'd ever been in and couldn't wait to run The National at Newark knowing I could do well. However, to say I ran it like an idiot would be an understatement; yes I ran it like an idiot. As usual, with all those winter miles in my legs I was strong, and because the course was reasonably flat I believed I could start easy and work through the field. The truth is that nobody, unless they're superman, which I wasn't, can start that far back and pass hundreds of runners in a packed field of over 1700 to work through the field. It should've been my best ever National, but it wasn't and so it's best forgotten.

Like many other things in life; we have to learn by our mistakes!

Two weeks later I made up for it by clocking 1:10:13 (recording PB's at 5 miles, 25.33 and 53.06 at 10) at Bath in the Half marathon. I felt so good after getting home that I ran four miles to stretch my legs. I was back on track and totally fired up for London.

Then with five weeks to go I was running fast laps round the Taylor Woodrow sports field when a pain under my right foot stopped me dead in my tracks; I was beginning to feel jinxed. Fortunately, that evening at a club meeting I bumped into Ron Jewkes again. He diagnosed the problem as a dropped arch, a mild form of Plantar Fasciitis, and advised me on how to treat it; which I did, and was back running easy after a few days before getting back in to the build up; gradually increasing mileage and pace. Unfortunately that injury meant missing another race: The Finchley 20. My body was telling me something so it wasn't worth taking the risk by running it. Five days later was Good Friday and the last chance to test myself in a hard race before London: it was The Maidenhead 10.

In the past, the Maidenhead course had been a bit suspect, insomuch that it was over distance, but it had been re-measured so as to be accurate; it just meant starting a bit further along the road. But there was nothing much they could do to make the long drag of a hill, which was synonymous with the event, any easier. After the enforced rest, I then tested myself by increasing the mileage leading up to Maidenhead, (94 miles including the race) I had nothing to lose and went hard from the gun, running 55:22 to finish 20th. I was happy with that, because at the time it was regarded as one of the toughest ten mile races in the area.

The week after was another high mileage week (106) and then over the final two weeks before London I tapered back, running 62 and 38 miles a week respectively; but was that taper enough? I wondered. I've never stopped asking myself that same question ever since.

Total mileage for the 15 week build up was 1080 despite, and annoyingly, losing eight training days. The weekly average was 72 miles; the highest, 106. Taking everything into consideration the build up had gone well, and the main thing was that I felt strong and confident of achieving my goal.

After a sleepless night I felt stressed and was full of nerves at the start of the race and worse still, by Tower Bridge I had tightened up considerably. 'It was just a bad patch, everybody goes them' I told myself, and got over it by not panicking, backing off the pace and relaxing before picking it up again and yet still only managing to run a disappointing 2:35:18.

It was a total anti-climax and as well as being drained emotionally I was physically shattered.

But I learnt a big lesson that day; never take anything for granted, especially when it involves running the marathon! Sub 2:30:00 had been my dream and the dream was in pieces. Having worked so hard for months I consoled myself to the fact that it just wasn't my day, and there really wasn't much I could do about it except pick myself up and start all over again.

After a miserable ride on the tube back to Ealing Broadway I suffered the nightmare of cramping up, again in both calf muscles, and as I was dragging myself up the station steps, using the handrail for support, a familiar voice behind me said mockingly 'Come on Peter, it's not that bad.' It was Les Smith. Les had spectated at the race and had travelled back on the same train as me. After loosening up on the short walk to his house, and a welcome cuppa, he took pity and drove me the couple of miles home where I suffered in silence, soaking in the comfort of a hot bath.

RECOVERING AND RELAXING

To thousands of other club runners up and down the country the day after London was just another training day. So after work I slipped my running kit on and ran laps on the grass of the Taylor Woodrow sports field...albeit very slowly; it was recovery time, physically and mentally. Getting over the disappointment of London didn't take too long and once I'd got it fully out of my legs and head I was back to normal training after about four weeks. The rest of the summer was spent racing mainly on the track, with mixed results.

A couple of weeks after the marathon, we, that's the family, spent a week holidaying in Devon, where, as well as playing about on the beach with the children I trained relaxed and easy.

Having lived in Cornwall I was always drawn back there, and so two weeks after the Devon holiday we were Cornwall bound again. Over the few days spent there I enjoyed some quality training, pushing myself hard along the quiet back roads around the town of Wadebridge, as well as off road on the disused rail line which had been turned in to a cycle track, The Camel Trail. I played with the children on the beaches in Cornwall too: Magic days.

Within hours of getting back from holiday I was competing in the Southern League, on the cinder track at Spike's Bridge which was completely clapped out, rock hard and rutted. In disgust I penned a rant in my training diary, 'Spike's Bridge track is a bloody disgrace and by the time a new one is laid I shall be too old anyway.' Too old; did I really mean that!

A week later at the beginning of July, on what was possibly the hottest day of the year (so far) I travelled by tube across London to Plaistow, standing much of the way, to run another Southern League 5000m. As I said, it was hotter than hell and because of the heat I mentally composed another of my plans. A few minutes before the start of the race I had a cold shower, but keeping my running kit on (except for my number, they were thin card in those days) and going to the line dripping wet, that was the first bit of the plan, which of course raised a few smiles; I smiled too. There was a slight breeze which did nothing to cool any of us down, as occasionally it blew clouds of dust up off the cinder track, but other than that, and the heat of course, I felt great; never better!

As the gun went I put the next part of my plan in to action; which was to sit at the back of the pack and keep an eye on things for the first few laps, then once fully loosened up and ready, to work through the field which had gone off at a suicidal pace, it was crazy; obviously those guys hadn't realised just how hot it really was (otherwise they'd have had cold showers too.) Sticking to the plan I continued to sit at the back until about half way, before passing the first of the tail enders. I couldn't believe how good I felt and hit the front with 800m to go, knowing I would win the race. Mike Barratt (who was wearing his track captains hat that day) was standing along the back straight and shouted 'Peter you can win this.' Which I did, scoring maximum points for the club as well as gaining great personal satisfaction with the individual win. I was buzzing. That victory was followed by another cold shower; minus kit. Winning that day was one of the greatest feelings of my running days; so too was that second cold shower; and there was no problem getting a seat on the tube going home; climbing the steps at Ealing Broadway station wasn't a problem either. Everything just clicked that day. I had faith in my plan and more importantly, total belief in myself. Oh yes; and true to form, I was our 'B' string runner.

Whereas winning is a great feeling, finishing last is the ultimate gut wrencher, it's a lousy feeling. That's what happened four weeks after

Plaistow. I was off to Devon again, but not for a holiday; it was to run in another Southern League meeting at Exeter. Once again I ran the 'B' string 5000m only to finish a very distant last, yet because conditions were ideal I couldn't put a finger on why I ran so badly; I'd felt like death all the way round the twelve and a half laps; it was awful. Maybe it was travel fatigue, who knows. No excuses, it was the same for everyone. There are days when everything clicks, whereas there are others when nothing does; and on that Saturday afternoon in Devon the 'B' string selection was justified.

Other than the disappointment of Exeter, winning had become a bit of a habit, well sort of, because during the weeks between Plaistow and Exeter I ran my last race in Taylor Woodrow colours, again over 5000m at West London Stadium, finishing second scorer in the winning team. Then at the beginning of September I was part of a four man Ealing team, who won the senior mens team race at the High Wycombe 'Furniture 5' mile road race. On the entry form it stated: 'Prizes in all races, mainly furniture in the senior races' And that's what we won, four comfortable armchairs, one each. And to this day I can't remember how we got them home; it certainly wasn't in the back of my Chevette.

It was on that day that I found out just how well built Thomas' pushchair was! After the race we were crossing the main road which was lined with parked vehicles, and as we edged forward, slowly and carefully, a car clipped the front of the push chair with Thomas in it. The car stopped immediately and the driver got out and apologised profusely, I assured him it was alright and off he went. And Thomas? He stirred, groaned and went back to sleep. And all the pushchair needed was a welding repair job to a hairline crack in the frame; once the job was done it was as good as new. That Silver Cross tubular steel model was, in those days the Volvo of pushchairs: I mean solid, not Swedish!

So, back to those prizes. Chairs made a change from medals or tee shirts, but money would've been handy. At the time it was never on any prize list except for elite athletes, and even then, any 'earnings' as such were deposited in to a Trust

Fund, to be used only for athletic related expenses. But how times have changed, and so they should. When other sports men and women are being paid obscene amounts, (tennis players and golfers are two examples that easily come to mind) consider then what our top distance runners earned in comparison for the work they've had to put in over the years just to get anywhere near the top; it was a pittance, except perhaps for those few at the very pinnacle.

With the majority of our top athletes it wasn't so much about the money (as many of them were working full time anyway) it was about training and competing. Distance runners love their sport and want nothing more than to just run. Don't take my word for it, ask any club runner, whether it's an aspiring teenager or an Olympic medallist. And while I'm on the subject of aspiring teenagers.......

JUNIORS ARE THE LIFEBLOOD

At about the same time as the Wycombe 5 I dipped my toe in to the water and put my coaches hat on for the first time. Although Ealing had a number of good track and field coaches, no-one seemed to be concentrating on coaching the junior distance runners, at least not that I was aware of.

Juniors are the lifeblood of any sport and as such should be encouraged, not only in the sport of their choice, the one they enjoy and excel in, they should also be given an opportunity to 'Multi-sport': give them the choice. That said, junior distance runners, who are usually as thin as sticks, ideally should focus on the non-contact sports, therefore reducing the risk of unnecessary injury. Ultimately, young runners should enjoy training and always thrive on competition. Enjoyment is the key that unlocks the door to success, and success was what some of the Ealing junior distance runners were achieving, and although they had performed well in school track competition during the summer, it was at cross country where they stood out from the crowd, gaining individual and team wins in Met. League and inter-club matches. For them, and for myself, 1984 had been generally successful and the future was looking bright.

There was however, in my personal life, a dark cloud forming which was beginning to cast an ominous shadow over me, which in due course would get darker.

I'd started a new job in September and never for one moment thought I'd made the wrong decision! The grass had looked greener, as it often does, especially in an interview situation, but from the word go and within the space of a few weeks it turned out not to be so green after all. I was still working in a training environment within the construction industry, but unlike the instructor's role, instead of a workshop, bricks and mortar, I had my own office, a secretary, a company car and on paper, the best job in the world. I honestly thought I was moving up. Unfortunately, in my bosses' eyes I wasn't moving anywhere; there was a definite personality clash from the word go. But I was determined not to let it get to me so I just kept my head down and got on with it the only way I knew how; by working hard and thinking positive.

Positive because it was Autumn and the cross country season was on the horizon and I was looking forward to it. The Met. League fixtures for 1984/85 followed much the same pattern as in previous seasons and would continue to do so for years to come. It was the same in cross country leagues across the country, where venues rotated and occasionally changed with new courses appearing on the fixture list, replacing any that had disappeared off the calendar completely, for whatever reason. It was simply another case of, 'If it ain't broke don't fix it.' There really are some things that don't need changing for the sake of it; cross country venues and fixtures being one of them.

June 1980 – Bourton on the Water 15
Wet to start – sun at the finish

October 1980 Horsenden Relays
The traditional start to the cross country season,
it wasn't always so dry.

1983 Hillingdon Round the Lido relay
Second fastest leg. The next day, January 1,
I went down with an injured hamstring.

May 1983 Evesham Half Marathon, on home soil

May 1984
2:35:18 I was devastateded

May 1984 Evesham Fun Run
On home territory again, I was flying. Then I ran the 4 miles home as a warm down.

1984, Southern League, Southall
Spikes Bridge Track – as hard as hell when it was dry; a quagmire when wet

May 1985 Evesham Half Marathon
71:01 13th place
The look on my face says it all, a sprint finish after 13 miles!

October 1985 Building Half Marathon
A bottle of bubbly beats a tee shirt!

April 1986 London Marathon
I ran it with a chest infection brought on by work related stress.

June 1987 Horsenden Hillingdon
Hills give strength. Through strength comes speed. Coaching: doing what I enjoy the most.

1985 CLUB CROSS COUNTRY CHAMPION

"Saturday, February 23rd Metropolitan League, Cranford. Congratulations Peter. If there is a club championship worth winning then this is the one and I'm over the moon. It was a beautiful day, sunny, with a south westerly breeze; good running weather. Due to the thaw it was sticky underfoot. The course was back through the narrow part of the woods, what I call the old course. Anyway, a bloody good afternoon. Race 5 (27:44) 34th. Warm up/down 5."

That was the entry in my training diary. The club cross country championships were contested over a number of designated races through the season, with points being awarded to the individual depending on the finishing position in each race. Then, at the end of the season the runner with the highest number of points was declared the winner.

I'd made up my mind at the start of the season to go all out to win it and on that day at Cranford, the last race of the championship, Rod Ainsworth and I were neck and neck on points, it was down to the wire. To win the title I had to beat him, and vice versa; no pressure there then.

The course was snooker table flat and on paper favoured the track runner. Rod was pretty swift over 800 and 1500m on the track and possessed a devastating finishing kick, so to beat him I had to get away to a flier from the gun; at least that was the plan. After an initial long lap the course crossed a narrow stream by way of an equally narrow wooden foot bridge which always caused a hold up, but I knew that by going eyeballs out from the start and crossing that bridge with the leaders, and in front of Rod, I could beat him; which I did; the plan had paid off. I was happy. Before the race I'd been quietly confident of winning (the club championship) knowing I was in good shape having beaten Rod in a Business House race on the country at Taylor Woodrow the previous weekend.

As always, the cross country season culminated with The National, at Milton Keynes, the week after Cranford. I was looking forward to it, although it wasn't a venue I was familiar with, and had no idea what to expect, which, at the time was just as well! After the juniors' races the course had become the usual sea of ankle deep mud for nine agonising miles that only got worse with each painful stride; walking the course and warming up had been a battle in itself. Words can't describe it; you had to be there. I, like everyone else, was covered in mud at the finish so didn't bother warming down, but instead made a bee line to the showers before the masses arrived, and before the drains in the showers slowly blocked, which they did. Consequently the overflow inched slowly towards the sports hall which was also the main changing area. But even with blocked drains those changing facilities were a world away from the tin baths at Parliament Hill. And unlike years later, in modern day cross country competition, there wasn't a club tent in sight; tent villages didn't exist.

Looking back on those 'big' field cross country championship races, it wasn't so much battling the elements or the sheer numbers that wore me down; it was the queueing in the funnels, waiting to be recorded while quietly whispering obscenities as numbness set in; but the post race banter brought the cynic out in me and the smiles to many. The mud in the funnels was as deep as it had been on the course, but as bad as conditions were, (and still are) competitors should always spare a thought for the officials, the unsung heroes of cross country. They too turn out in all weathers when they could be at home, feet up in front of a warm fire. But, just like the runners, in a perverse sort of way officials must also enjoy it to endure turning out week after week, year after year.

Is the cross country fraternity, including officials, really a masochistic brotherhood?

The summer was once again divided between competing on the track and the road. But unlike previous years it seemed that the cross country season had started earlier than usual, in mid-September, with the road season dragging on well in to October which was when I ran The Building Half Marathon at Welwyn Garden City. I hadn't trained specifically for it which was something I always did when racing distances over ten miles, so I treated it more as a training run, which was something else I never did. I believe that a race is a test, an end to a means (whereas training is a means to an end) where the objective is to get the best out of yourself by running as fast as you can for as long as you can over the given distance; pushing beyond the boundaries, so to speak. In that particular instance there was a valid reason for delaying specific preparation and leaving the decision to run until the last minute; that reason was because only ten days before the race I'd had a vasectomy operation. Whoops.

Racing a half marathon so soon after the operation wasn't the wisest thing I'd ever done, so I took it easy(ish) especially on the downhill stretches, recording a time of 76.05. I'd ran in company colours, and because I was the first company man to finish I was rewarded for my effort and presented with a bottle of champagne by one of the marketing girls, that was as well as receiving the obligatory race medal. Maybe I should've asked for a pay rise!

I'd taken a calculated risk by running that day, and thankfully everything was intact in the nether regions at the finish, I did though feel a bit tender for a few days after. So taking that into consideration I gave myself the luxury of completely resting the following day. That days rest was enough to recharge the batteries and after a couple of weeks of light training I was back to normal.

I loved running half marathons! The Building Half was one of three I ran during the year. The first was at Evesham on the early May Bank Holiday which also incorporated an away day for the club. We hired a coach, filled it, and everyone, especially me, had a good time. Some of my family turned out to give their support. I'd ran 77:17 over the same course two years earlier, yet despite its challenging terrain I smashed that time by over 6 minutes finishing 13th to record 71:01.

We were holidaying in the West Country in September so I took the opportunity to run at Dawlish. Like Evesham and Welwyn, the Dawlish half was not conducive for fast times as the course could be, at best, described as seriously undulating. Knowing Devon to be a county famous for its rolling countryside and breathtaking coast line I phoned the race organiser and asked 'What's the course like, is it hilly?' 'Slightly undulating,' was his reply. To me slightly undulating means flattish with a few gentle contours; like hell it was.

As the field headed away from the start in Dawlish town centre, almost immediately we hit the first serious climb, and what a test of strength that was; best described as scaling the Dawlish equivalent to the north face of the Eiger; and a taste of things to come later in the race! When racing over longer distances I normally took the first couple of miles easy as a way of warming in to it, before settling down to my stride. The theory being that it's better to be patient early on, therefore saving energy for later when it's needed most. Many runners who dash off from the gun find it impossible to sustain that adrenaline rush to the finish, thirteen long miles away. It's a great feeling, passing those who had gone off too fast at the start, as they tire and drift backwards. On the other hand, there is nothing more demoralising than being passed as the finish comes into sight, when the mind is dead and the legs can't respond.

Just before the start at Dawlish, I'd been chatting to a guy from London, Ealing in fact, and as luck would have it he was running unattached. He pulled away from me early on and I let him go, but after a few miles and some undulations later, I passed him to open up a 20 second gap at the finish. We chatted again and it wasn't long after that, that he joined us. That's what comes of talking to strangers at races.

100% STRESS BUSTER

And getting back to that rift and the stress of work it really was a no win situation knowing there was no turning back. I was living in the hope that things would improve having developed excellent working relationships with senior site and office personnel, college, polytechnic and university professionals, and last but not least, the company trainees who I was directly responsible for; but the one who really mattered most, my immediate boss, was the one who was sticking the knife in. It was obvious that forging a mutual working relationship with him was impossible, yet despite doing all I could to make it work, it proved to be a fruitless task. So running not only remained the sport I loved, but it also became my salvation; a 100% stress buster, as it cleared my mind of the negatives, allowing me to focus on the positives.

In the meantime I was enjoying the coach/mentor role and the way some club members, not just juniors, were responding to my methods and the sessions I was putting together. Their progress made everything worthwhile as they continued to enjoy and benefit from the training; it was a win win situation.

Those words: enjoy, enjoyed, enjoying and enjoyment sum up everything that running gives, because there is no point in continuing to do something and not enjoy it. Perhaps that's how I should have resolved the work situation, after all, to every problem there is a solution, and the solution in that case would have been to take the bull by the horns and left, instead of prolonging the agony in the hope it would go away, but, of course, it didn't, and things just went from bad to worse; but at least running didn't. Under the circumstances it had been a good year, as I'd raced regularly over the country, on the track and on the road; yet most importantly and despite the stress, I'd kept injury free.

And there was also some great news for the club. During the summer Ealing council had been given the go-ahead to build an eight lane all weather track in Perivale Park. The money had been allocated and companies were invited to tender for the building of it; exciting times ahead then.

ATHLETICS WEEKLY

Working with Mike opened my eyes to the amount of hard work needed to get some of the lads to turn out and run cross country, especially the league and championship races. They had to be pinned down and almost forced to swear on oath that they would compete. Not only was it hard work pinning them down, it was also very time consuming. Hours were spent on the phone chasing round; and there was no such thing as the internet then. When it came to running in open races and entering themselves there just wasn't the hassle; they just did it because it was easy! Events countrywide were advertised in the runners' bible: Athletic's Weekly.

Open in that context meant anyone could enter as long as they met the organisers' criteria; athletes simply chose their event and paid the appropriate entry fee. It was a straightforward process and done through the post by simply enclosing the necessary personal details, a cheque and a stamped addressed envelope which, once received, all relevant race information, including the race number, was sent by return of post. There were some race organisers who accepted entries on the day (or evening) when numbers were collected at the venue. Both systems were simple, and they worked.

As well as advertising future events, AW as it was affectionately known, published race results and reports, interviews, features, book reviews, classified ads. obituaries, and more. If it had anything to do with athletics it was odds on that information could be found within its pages.

Despite the friction at work the year ended on a real high with the intention being to continue through 1986 regardless of any barriers!

The years' total mileage: 2829. Weekly average: 54.5. Highest week 76.5.

1986 RUNNING A MARATHON FOR FUN REALLY!

Against the odds, 1985 had been a good year, therefore I saw no reason why 1986 wouldn't go the same way.

On the strength of my 1984 London Marathon time I entered the 1986 event and benefited from not having to go through the ballot, leaving me free to enjoy injury free training, in the meantime everything (other than work) was fine. I'd raced almost every week during January and was really fired up and ready to run a good Southern at Brighton.

It was a straightforward drive from London and we were making good time until, and with not far to go, the traffic in front, without warning stopped; and so did I, but the car behind me didn't. Smash. It was the classic shunt, but thankfully at low speed. The impact pushed me in to the back of the car in front, a very solid stationary Mercedes; oh hell. By instinct, and on impact, I'd checked the rear view mirror and to my horror saw the car behind bearing down on me, there was no way he was stopping. It all happened in slow motion, or at least that's how it seemed; I'd braced myself and waited for the crunch. Thankfully there were no injuries and no real structural damage to the car; at least it was still driveable even though the front was a real mess with the headlights totally smashed; which meant no Southern for me. After exchanging insurance details I turned the car round and drove home. But at least the day wasn't written off entirely and because it was still light when I got back I got rid of my frustration by running eyeballs out round the golf links and through the blanket of snow that covered them: but oh what a day!

And the car. It was a company car and as I was working out my redundancy notice my boss was not the happiest man in the world when I knocked on his door on Monday morning to break the news. The air turned blue and the fan changed colour; metaphorically speaking. Up to that point our relationship had been frosty to say the least, but on that Monday morning it completely froze over.

TOWN MOOR

And while on the subject of freezing over! I'd never been to Newcastle upon Tyne, but there's a first time for everything. All I knew was it's in the north east of England, a long way from London, and that the city was hosting The National, which was also the first of the races in my eight week build up to the London Marathon in April.

The Southern Counties Athletic's Association chartered a train for the journey to Newcastle and Ealing were allocated seats in one of the first class carriages; which was real luxury.

Hundreds of runners (soft southerners as we were referred to by the tough north easterners) piled off the train and made the trek from Central Station up Northumberland Street to the course at the Town Moor, stopping en-route at the changing facilities which were in the civic centre covered car park. But the first thing that really hit me getting off the train was just how cold it was. The station acted as a wind tunnel; and still does. Imagine then the bemused looks of the Saturday shoppers as the throng snaked its way through their midst.

Despite being close to the centre of a major industrial city, my first impression of the Town Moor was just how exposed it was, almost like being out in the country, Siberia upon Tyne. The bitterest wind imaginable chilled the bones, and worse, dotted around the course frozen water formed mini lakes under solid ice in places, with snow and more ice forming crusts in others; but those crusts and frozen ice were soon broken up once the first races started. It was nine miles, three laps of pure hell with two steep climbs, in close proximity, on each lap, known locally as 'Cow Hill' (appropriately named because of the cattle that graze there, but not on that day). I wanted to forget it but never would, and I'd never forget meeting the Morpeth Harrier legend and fellow bricklayer, Jim Alder. That was at the finish, after queueing through the funnels when everyone was cursing the cold, with chattering teeth and runny noses. Jim and I got chatting, small talk really, before I asked him where the best place was to get a pint of decent local beer, before catching the train? He recommended a spit and sawdust bar which was only a stone's throw from the station. 'Ask for a pint of wallop,' he said. Which I did. I was with Rod and we downed a couple each, those pints didn't touch the sides and it was good stuff.

As I never ran particularly well in the big cross country championships I knew Town Moor would be no different, and it wasn't, but as well as the cold, the wind and all that stuff, I'll remember the day forever, with a certain fondness and a smile.

By the time I'd got back to the covered car park the mud had dried and stuck to my legs, so the priority was to get in the shower quick, before another queue formed. The shower was a khaki canvas tent rigged up outside the car park entrance, and although a bit primitive with no lighting, at least the water was hot. But, surprise, surprise, there was the usual post race banter coming from the dark crowded steamy interior; crowded or not I squeezed in, and did the necessary without dropping my soap, which in the gloom would've been a disaster; but it was good to be clean again.

The three hour train journey to King's Cross was scheduled non-stop; except for one, and that was to drop the Verlea boys off at Stevenage, but it didn't stop until it got to London. Those Verlea boys were not amused, then neither would I have been; but everyone else seemed to see the funny side. More banter!

And the winner that day was a soft southerner: Tim Hutchings of Crawley AC; with Dave Clarke and Eamonn Martin, also soft southerners, second and third respectfully. Tipton Harriers, from the Midlands won the coveted team prize. Soft southerners indeed!

As the train sped south I reflected on my day in Newcastle, never thinking for one moment that in the distant future the north east would play a significant part in the twilight years of my life, especially where athletics was concerned.

CHEST INFECTION

Anyway, back to the build up for The London. The eight week build up was interrupted on and off by short bouts of illness, with the worst coming ten days before the race. I'd been consistently coughing through the week, right up to the weekend before the marathon. It was on that weekend when, almost at the end of my final long Sunday run that I started coughing and wheezing non-stop again, and worse; breathing became so difficult that I had to walk the final mile home. With a week to go that was the last thing I needed.

I saw the doctor the following morning who diagnosed a chest infection and prescribed antibiotics. I asked her if it was okay to run the marathon 'No, you shouldn't be running anywhere with a chest infection,' then with a smile she asked 'Could you walk it instead?' I returned the smile and said 'Yes I could.' She signed me off work for a week, wished me good luck and with that I was on my way.

I'm not sure if she remembered that it was her who, indirectly, had started me off running in the first place. It was even harder to believe that that had been over eight years previous and that I'd gone from being addicted to cigarettes to being addicted to running! I'd become a running junkie!

I ran London, albeit slowly, and just for fun, but not in fancy dress or any of that stuff; it wasn't that sort of fun. With the doctor's words ringing in my ears I went through the first few miles at a very leisurely seven to eight minute mileing pace, which in its own way was similar to walking (just as the doctor had suggested.) I held myself right back until the Cutty Sark which is almost all down hill from the start, with the occasional flat stretches which is where many go off too fast only to blow up later; which I didn't. Knowing I was running nowhere close to a PB, which wasn't the intention anyway, I really did run for fun and soaked up the support from the crowds. There was no pressure, no stress and certainly no ill effects from the chest infection; I just relaxed and focused on finishing.

It wasn't until years later that I was made aware of the dangers of running with a chest infection; especially running twenty six miles; no wonder the doctor asked if I could walk it. Had I known the real dangers I wouldn't have done it at all; walking or running.

Once I'd finished, meeting Phil at the chaos of the finish area was my concern, he was my lift home. I took a calculated guess that he'd finish close to me; actually I was hoping we'd cross the line together, after all, we'd trained together often enough. With the finish in sight I slowed up along Birdcage Walk in the hope of seeing him, but didn't, and ran on to clock 2.53.39 in what would be my last marathon; although I didn't know it at the time.

Phil didn't keep me waiting long; his time read exactly 2.54.00 as he ran under the gantry clock. On the way home we stopped along the embankment, near the World's End estate, for a well earned beer; after all, alcohol dulls pain and eases stiffness, Phil's words not mine, but I believe him; and although we weren't drinking wallop, just like wallop it was good ale: Fuller's London Pride.

The biggest kick I got out of that day was fulfilling my sponsorship pledge by raising over a thousand pounds for Coston's First School. It was used to buy computer equipment for the pupils; my Clare being one of them, and who, with some of her school mates, parents and teachers, were in the Mall cheering me on as I ran past, them waving and me waving back. It was a very emotional feeling.

And just like the Monday after the Southern my boss was not very happy, 'going sick and running the marathon,' he said. Those words meant there were more nails in the proverbial coffin.

The remaining six weeks in the job could have been really stressful, but running was my saviour, and as long as I could run I was stress free.

Having left all that stuff behind I was thankful to have lost the weight off my mind, and so with my bricklaying tools over my shoulder I started work on a building site: The Waterglade Centre, in Ealing Broadway. I'd come full circle since my apprenticeship days as a teenager in the sixties.

I hadn't been on site for years, at least not to work, and had completely lost touch with just how hard working in the construction industry really was. It was due to the nature of bricklaying and the physical graft that went with it that caused the injury that brought my competitive running days to a premature end, but I didn't realise it at the time and life carried on much the same. I did though reduce mileage, training and racing, which gave my body a chance to recover from the shock of switching from sedentary office based work to the outdoor world of hard manual labour.

As the summer heat slowly subsided to be replaced by the cool of autumn, training was frequently interrupted by intermittent hamstring pain. Nothing like that had happened before and was frustrating as it came and went without warning, forcing whole chunks of training to be lost and, because the pain wasn't constant, I became concerned when it didn't respond to the usual treatment of ice and stretching, so I knew it couldn't be a straightforward hamstring pull. The bizarre thing was there were times when running at pace I was completely pain free, so I really was at a loss to know exactly what it was. Typically, I did what most runners did in the same situation - I ignored the pain as much as I could and ran through it hoping it would go away. Of course it didn't. I learnt to live with it, running when I could, right up to the end of the year. Holding with the Christmas day tradition I turned up at the Hillingdon club house with a wrapped gift.

The reduced mileage reflects what an up and down year it had been, but in the bigger scheme of things it could've been so much worse. I was thankful to be working and not totally crippled, and at least I was able to run between the periods of enforced rest.

Total Mileage for the year: 2141.5. Weekly average: 41. Highest weekly: 70.

1987: A NEW TRACK

After the disappointment of 1986 I was determined to make the most of 1987 and devoted more time to coaching the juniors who had improved considerably due to their consistent training, and to make sure that trend continued I hatched another plan to make sure it did. I would fit coaching in between my own spasmodic training, and because I was running fewer miles it was easy to do. Therefore, Monday evenings were devoted to junior group training; seniors were invited too.

During the summer, all sessions were on grass, alternating between Horsenden Hill, for the development of power and strength whereas Berkeley fields was undulating and ideal for continuous running at pace, and fartlek. Perivale Park was totally flat and perfect for pure speed work. The sessions were unstructured and different to anything they'd ever done before, so everyone was curious as well as enthusiastic, but above all, training was enjoyable and the improvement in form, technique and success in competition was noticeable.

I was frequently asked 'Peter, where's the best place to train?' My answer then, as it always would be, was, 'It's not where you train, it's how you train'. The sessions worked then and would still work many years later, with minor adjustments depending on the age range of the group. Enjoyment then, as it always should be now, is the key to successful training and competition.

When the clocks changed to signal the onset of winter, we moved off the grass to do hill sesisons at Studland Road, Hanwell. The hill was well lit, relatively traffic free, quiet and within easy distance from the club house which meant the group could run there and be warmed up ready to start the session on arrival: Studland Road was a brute of a hill. The efforts were set in distance and intensity and catered for all age groups and different abilities. Anyone who ran those sessions will, I'm sure, remember them with affection and a wry smile. Just like Horsenden Hill, the efforts were designed to give not only strength and power, but also to develop mental toughness; which they did.

Although I'd missed most of the cross country season, I felt in reasonable enough shape and joined a large group of the clubs' distance runners and entered the Bath Half marathon in March. Once again, we did what most clubs do when travelling long distances and hired a coach and everyone looked forward to the day out. I was hoping to run a decent(ish) time as only two weeks before I'd run 76 minutes in the Southall half marathon, over a tough undulating course. Because of the dodgy hamstring there hadn't been the usual preparation, but more importantly there hadn't been any pain either.

I was in good spirits on the journey to Bath and looked forward to just enjoying the race and the day in general. However, my diary entry records a totally different story: "Bath Half Marathon. Pain up the back of the leg at 3 miles forced me to pull out at 5. Back to square one; can I ever win!' Needless to say I wasn't in such good spirits on the journey home. It was obvious: I didn't stretch my legs after getting home that time.

Booking in to the Athletes' Clinic at Hillingdon Hospital was a formality. A GP's referral wasn't necessary as all it took was a phone call to make the appointment. After some delicate poking, prodding and acute pain, the problem was diagnosed as a slipped disc; specifically the fifth lumbar of the vertebrae; oh bugger. Based on our discussion the doctor and I traced the cause back to some particularly heavy lifting when I was working on site, and although it hadn't been detected then, continuous running had exacerbated the problem; and then bang, the disc had popped and whacked the sciatic nerve, which manifested itself as a hamstring injury. Traction was the immediate treatment, daily for a week, then further exercises for an indefinite period and definitely no running. All in all I was out for two months, then in mid May came the phone call I'd been waiting for, Dr. Sperryn gave me the all clear to start running again. That was great news and meant I was back on the long road to fitness. Although I'd been out for all that time I was still coaching and enjoying Monday evenings at the club house and because it was summer we were training on the grass again. And with regards my own training: I was managing, but with no real pace; it just felt good being able to run again, albeit very slowly and over no real distance, at least not to start with. It was after four months of gradual progress that I got back to something that resembled any level of fitness and because there had been no further leg pain I felt in good enough shape to race, so I did; starting with a 10k road race in Battersea Park at the beginning of August, and later in the month 5000m. on the waterlogged cinders at Spike's Bridge. Although the times were diabolically slow it didn't matter, I was happy to be getting back into shape and things were looking up; then the worst thing that could happen did! It was on August Bank Holiday Monday.

I'd taken a group out for what was the last grass session of the summer; but during the evening what had started as a slightly sore achilles tendon gradually got worsened and became the sort of pain associated with someone sticking a knife in to it; to a runner that's the worst sort of pain. After a few days of continually icing it I tried jogging again but it was no good. I stopped running altogether and didn't start again until mid November.

Achilles tendons are bad news, so why, as we evolved as a species have we been lumbered with the damn things! So what with a knackered back and dodgy tendons I was in a real mess.

As the year came to a premature and disappointing end for me personally, it marked a milestone for Ealing and Southall Athletic Club, because on October 11th. an eight lane all weather track was officially opened in Perivale Park by 1992 Olympic 100m sprint gold medallist Linford Christie, and 1984 Olympic javelin champion Tessa Sanderson. The track hadn't been built exclusively for the club, but it did become its base, and a club house was built some years later. For the time being Monday evenings at Pitshanger Park was still the place to be seen running, or as in my case, not running!

The year fizzled out like a damp squib, and although I turned up at Ruislip on Christmas Day my heart wasn't in it. I just went through the motions, put on a brave face, smiled, shook a few hands, wished everyone a Merry Christmas then went home.

In November I turned forty to become a first year veteran. That being the case there was one club trophy I wanted and was determined to win, even though the odds were stacked against me. However, if life really does begin at forty, as the saying goes, then I was going to put it to the test; the proof of the pudding would definitely be in the eating. Having written the year off as far as my own running was concerned, I became the club's self appointed supporter in chief, travelling to, and shouting myself hoarse at races. Supporting was the next best thing to running; old habits die hard!

1988: MOVING ON

The new year started where the old one left off; with reduced mileage, rest, illness, injury, treatment and the occasional run, and I was still shouting myself hoarse at races as often as I could, which was very often. I saw out the cross country season by spending a pain free day at Newark, the scene of my 1984 National disaster! A few weeks later, but on firmer ground, I was spectating again, at the London Marathon. As it had been in 1984 it was just the Olympic selection race with Kevin Forster qualifying with another 2nd place overall. It was a repeat of 1984, when he finished behind the winner Charlie Spedding; who went on to win the bronze medal in the Los Angeles Olympic Marathon.

I left the marathon that day with renewed energy and motivation wondering if I would ever get back to my pre-1987 fitness. I was feeling positive, yet apprehensive at the same time; it's a strange feeling! The London Marathon is a great event, whether competing or spectating; I was content to enjoy the day as a spectator and left there inspired. Inspiration, especially self inspiration, like enjoyment, can be everything we need to get us back on our feet.

It wasn't until June that I dared test myself, which I did by running in a London League 10k road race at Harrow recording 37:29 which left me feeling a bit flat, having ran a 10k PB of 32.50 on the same course in 1985; but then maybe I was being a bit hard on myself.

After some decent spells of training, five weeks later I ran another London League 10k. in Battersea Park knocking almost a minute off the Harrow time. 'Not great, but at least things were moving in the right direction, towards the light that was definitely at the end of the long dark tunnel' I thought. Although the omens weren't good there was no way I was giving up; especially when there was a trophy to be won.......but I was also on the move.

ON THE TRACK

By the beginning of June I was living and working in Swindon, travelling home to the family at weekends, and for the occasional evening during the week. It was on one of those evening visits that I took the opportunity to race 3000m on the new Ealing track, surprising myself by finishing five seconds off my 3k PB on virtually no training and coming second to my good friend, New Zealander, Bernard Orsman. who I'd been advising on a regular basis, and which he took advantage of that evening. Sadly though, it was the last time I ever competed on that track - on any track in fact. That time though, was an indicator as to how my fitness was returning, incredibly, and on low mileage.

Although the permanent house move to Swindon was imminent I'd already been preparing mentally for the forthcoming cross country season and specifically to the winning of that club trophy.

During the summer evenings my training runs were used not only to keep in shape, but also as a way of discovering Swindon and the surrounding countryside without getting lost. They were mainly out and back runs, at least until I got my bearings, and things were looking up. I was running reasonably well and pain free, but maybe

I was being naïve in thinking the injury that had caused me so much frustration for so long was at last, a thing of the past; I kept my fingers crossed.

SWINDON HARRIERS

On Wednesday evenings a group of distance runners from Swindon Harriers met for their mid-week steady run, covering anything between 6 and 10 miles and I joined them. Steady runs? Those guys were no different to other serious runners, because although the intention was to keep it steady, the reality was exactly the opposite as the competitive nature of each one, including me, kicked in. Inevitably, the pace increased so that by half way, the steady run had become a furious burn up back to base (at the County Ground) just as the Monday evenings at Ealing had been.

In mid October the family upped sticks and made the move to Swindon, and although it was over a hundred and twenty miles (or thereabouts) round trip along the M4 to London I was still a member of Ealing and Southall and eligible to compete for the one club championship that would give me the cross country double. Having won the club senior championship in the 1984/85 season now the intention was to win the veteran's award, I'd never get another chance. Training had been inconsistent due to the move and all that stuff, but confidence was high and I was determined to win it, which I did; and unlike the last time, it didn't go down to the wire. It was a farewell gesture, my personal swan song and my success; I'd achieved what I'd set out to achieve.

Ealing and Southall Athletic Club had been a massive part of my life for over ten years, where I'd gone through the highs and lows, accepting all challenges head on as a determined and dedicated club runner. In my quest for success I had always given my best and couldn't ask anymore of myself; but the time really had come to move on.

Joining Swindon Harriers was never the same, it couldn't be. Moving there from Ealing was very difficult and furthermore, the sciatica pain came and went at irregular intervals, more frequently and without warning which meant I'd never get back to full running fitness; and although I still enjoyed those Wednesday runs, I was flat and my heart just wasn't in it.

1989/90 THE YEARS OF TRUTH

Looking back over the years I was proud of what I'd achieved at Ealing, and had looked forward to doing the same as a veteran at Swindon; but it didn't happen, and there was no magic solution. I occasionally competed for them but it didn't take long to realise I was only making up the numbers and rarely scored for the team, whether on the road or the country, knowing that I was only running for fun. But hell, that's what I'd been doing since that first day, years ago in Ravenor Park; but truthfully, running just to make up the numbers isn't a lot of fun.

To compliment the reduction in mileage I bought a road bike and discovered more of the Wiltshire countryside, covering many more miles than I ever could by running; I even competed in a couple of local time trials. By mixing running and cycling I was getting the best of both worlds, but knew that one day I'd be confronted with the harsh reality, which became apparent, especially after the many visits to my osteopath friend and neighbour, Mike. I was spending more time on his treatment table than I was either running or cycling. It was on one of those visits that he finally hit me with the brutal truth, 'Peter, if you keep running as you are doing, sooner or later your disc will pop completely, leaving bone on bone, and that'll mean surgery.' Mike's warning, just as the doctor's had been years before was enough; so I drastically reduced the mileage I was doing and with a heavy heart gave up competitive running forever.

AND FINALLY

Having given up competitive running didn't mean I'd given running up completely. I was getting out occasionally, jogging relaxed and easy, much of it on grass. It was a way of keeping in shape, and although I enjoyed cycling it couldn't compare with the enjoyment I still got from running, it didn't even get close; and honestly, rear wheel punctures were a real pain in the backside.

Since moving to Swindon, over the years my life became a mess, at home and at work. In 1995 I went through a divorce and started a new life with Pam, and although she wasn't sporty, that soon changed as I 'retired' the road bike for it to be replaced with mountain bikes; we became lycra clad social cyclists, at home and abroad.

Although life was good, there was something missing, but I couldn't quite put a finger on what that something was; that was until May of Millennium year which was when the penny dropped. We'd spent a week holidaying on the beautiful Greek island of Kefalonia, the setting for the novel and movie, Captain Corelli's Mandolin. After reading it my life changed forever! Great book; lousy film.

Since childhood I've loved painting and all things art, and that's what was missing; from dabbling in paint on and off for so many years I became a full time artist living out my childhood dream in Argostoli, the capital of the island, the island I often refer to as paradise. The plan, yes, yet another, was to spend the summer there, to paint, to sell them, then return to England at the end of the holiday season, in late October; which I did, but it wasn't October 2001, it was six and a half years later, in October 2007 and it wasn't back home.

Having decided against moving back to England, and with Pam being a Francophile, France seemed the most obvious place to settle, so we did. While there (and after almost twenty years) I put my coaches hat back on and didn't need to speak French to do it; sign language and a whistle was enough to get the message across, and anyway, Jerome, the man I was coaching spoke good English. Settling in France had figured in our long term plans and for a while it worked; but the saying is true, 'there's no place like home, it's where the heart is.' The upside was I wouldn't need to learn a new language, or, because we were moving to the north east of England; perhaps I just might!!!

Pam was born in County Durham, so in the winter of 2010 we dug up our shallow French roots and headed for the city of Durham, having decided it was the place to settle for the long haul?

With the packing boxes empty and the house ship shape, it was in the Spring of 2011 that I headed to the Graham Sports Centre, the home of

Durham University sports and Durham City Harriers' base camp, to put my coaching skills in to practice; initially working with Max Coleby's group before moving to assist Bryan Mackay.

THE JUNIOR GRASS GROUP

It was though, only a matter of time before it happened! Bryan sensed I was getting itchy feet and in 2014 I formed The Junior Grass Group. The group consisted of junior distance runners, aged between ten and eighteen, boys and girls, who trained on grass; hence the name. So as not to appear ageist the group has always been open to all club members whatever their age or gender; Durham university students were also welcome. Over the years some drifted in and gave it a try, but no senior harriers ever did?

Although the group trained on grass, many have achieved team and individual success on the track, road and cross country, but especially cross country. That though wasn't the sole reason why they trained on grass and the group wasn't formed specifically to run cross country.

Running on grass is similar to running on a protective carpet with thick underlay, it absorbs the impact that foot plant can have on the body, therefore reducing the risk of injury that too much running on unforgiving surfaces such as the track and road can cause growing adolescents. Juniors, as they grow, naturally become stronger, then as they do, is the time when they can gradually vary the surfaces to train and race on.

Many of the group ran in junior and Comprehensive Inter-Schools competition, before becoming eligible for selection to compete in the Cross Country Cup and the English Schools, which are both national championship events.

At club level they graduated to the mud, sweat and tears of the The North East Harrier League, with its quirky slow and fast pack handicap system, which, as far as I'm aware, (although I could be wrong) is unique, insomuch that it is the only cross country league in the country to adopt that system.

It's well known that the Grass Group love running cross country and as well as the Harrier League, couldn't wait to run in the championship events: The North East counties, the Northern area and The National, which were all straight races (meaning there were no packs or handicap system) which put them on a level playing field, so to speak.

To club juniors, especially those in the group, the pinnacle of junior success was earning the right to wear the coveted Durham County purple hoodie by qualifying for, and competing in The National Schools Cross Country Championships, which is the junior equivalent of the senior National event. Unlike their senior counterparts however, juniors had to run three qualifying races: Durham City Schools; Durham County Schools and Northern Inter-county schools, to compete in The National.

Under normal circumstances, that is, weather permitting, there were six Harrier League fixtures, plus the Sherman Cup (for men and boys) and the Davison Shield (for women and girls.) to add to the schools events which made the juniors fixture list heavily congested. And if that wasn't enough occasionally grass group junior(s) have been selected to run in the prestigious Inter-Counties

Championships, a race which always fell on the weekend before the National Schools. It's not possible to peak 100% for both, although some have tried and fallen short on both counts!

My take on that dilemma is that The Inter-Counties will always be there for future years as juniors become seniors, because whichever way you look at it, their years at school are limited to age, and before you know it school is over. So, having taken that in to consideration I have always advised and encouraged those in the group to enjoy their school years while they can and concentrate on doing well in The National Schools and other school competitions. Coaches, and that's not just me, can only advise on what we think is best.

Running with The Junior Grass Group could be looked upon as the start of an enjoyable journey of discovery; from the age of ten, or thereabouts, then typically progressing through junior and comprehensive school, sixth form, university and beyond, to wherever destiny takes them in the wide world.

One thing though is certain, like me, they will never forget their time with The Junior Grass Group.

PART TWO

THE A 2 Z OF COACHING JUNIOR DISTANCE RUNNERS

As humans we are born to run, and there is no more living proof than in junior athletes; boys and girls. For them it's natural, because from a very early age they run everywhere, and, what's more, as soon as they're old enough they want to compete.

The selection and interpretation of the following 'buzz' words in this A 2 Z are my own and personal. There are of course, many other words I could have chosen, and I'm sure there are coaches, distance runners, juniors and seniors, who will look at my selection and compare them with their own, ultimately, it's down to personal choice; because what's important to one may not be so important to another. But just as in the wide range of coaching skills and training methods, there are no hard and fast rules. It's what makes athletics, and in particular distance running, so rewarding and enjoyable, both as a competitor and coach. Enjoyment is the key to success: achieving what you set out to achieve, which, as everyone by now knows; is my definition of the word success.

ABILITY: All junior distance runners have ability, for some it's natural, whereas there are others who have to work a bit harder to achieve the same results; and that's the key, working just that bit harder! Having all the natural ability in the world counts for nothing if the athlete is not prepared to work at it. If you think you can't you won't; if you believe you can you will.

BELIEF: junior runners should believe in themselves and what they want to achieve, there's nothing wrong with that, in fact it should be encouraged and nurtured slowly and not forced by anyone, especially the coach. Most juniors enjoy the challenge and adrenaline rush of competition, especially when they're winning.

COMMUNICATION: *Communicate*: to share or exchange information or ideas (Concise Oxford

Dictionary). The relationship between coach and athlete has to be two way, based on communication and trust; from working on training schedules to planning competition. It's also important that parents are supportive, to the athlete and the coach.

Working on training schedules should be two way, and because they're on-going must be reviewed periodically. The schedules should be flexible and not set in stone so as to be easily adjusted at short notice for whatever the reason. On the other hand, planning future competition can be a very frustrating time as coach and athlete try and balance between racing for school and club.

Here's an interesting scenario: One of the most talented juniors to come through the grass group was selected to run for Durham in the U/20's race at the Inter-Counties Championships at Loughborough, having already qualified to run The National Schools Championships at Leeds the week after. Being in the upper sixth form meant it was his last chance to compete in the schools and on current form he'd run very well, but against all advice, not just mine, he ran both.

As he walked towards me from the finish funnel at Leeds his body language said it all, then without prompting, he said "Peter, the Inter-Counties was still in my legs." He didn't need to say any more as I knew just how he felt. Those things happen, and hopefully a lesson was learnt.

Had he concentrated on the schools race he'd have finished his years of school competition on a high note. However, because of his immense talent and mental strength he would surely qualify for the inter-counties in future years. It was a case of communication breakdown where the athlete questioned his coaches judgement; a Judgement based on learning and experience. It takes years of competition for an athlete to be able to peak for two major cross country races within the space of a week, if it's possible at all, years that many juniors just haven't had the time to develop.

DISTANCE: The question is often asked, 'What is the maximum distance juniors should run?' The answer is, 'Because of the physiological differences between individuals there are no hard and fast rules; in this instance it's down to common sense.' Boys and girls from as young as ten, with the correct training, should be able to run continuously for at least thirty minutes or more; depending on the pace. However, as those same runners get older, stronger and faster, they'll run further in the same time, and faster over the same distance, through the years of adolescence to physical and mental maturity.

As far as racing is concerned juniors should proceed with caution! Don't race too far, too soon or too often. Concentrate on the middle distance events, 800m, 1500m. and even 3000m. Cross country race distances vary and are set for different age groups. Once again common sense should prevail.

When juniors train and race regularly over longer distances through their years of growth, they risk muscular and skeletal injury as well as mental burn out. They must be patient and not overdo it; it's not worth taking the risk.

ENJOYMENT: For junior distance runners, every run, training session and every race should be an enjoyable experience, despite the pain. Pain is an integral part of the sport and takes some getting used to. But as well as pain there should also be the feeling of exhilaration. I've often heard juniors muttering under their breath "I enjoyed that session" even though they were on their knees when they said it.

When the sessions are enjoyable, the group, or the individual, will always be back for more, knowing there will be icing on the cake! That icing could be the enjoyment of winning a race or setting a personal best, or being part of a team win. Runners who aren't prepared to endure pain as part of the enjoyment should take up something that doesn't hurt; dominoes or darts spring to mind.

FORM: Form, generally speaking refers to the co-ordination of a runner in perfect motion, from the poise of the head to the relaxed smoothness of the arm swing, the upright stance of the torso to the knee lift and foot plant. The athlete's form should be smooth and graceful, so much so that running appears effortless to the onlooker.

GROWTH: Growing is natural, but for many junior distance runners, with growth comes a degree of uncertainty, because at around the age of ten upwards, especially for boys, it is the time when growth 'spurts' are triggered, that's instead of the steady growth which they've been used to. Suddenly they shoot upwards, and unfortunately that sudden spurt can often be accompanied by pain and aching joints. Thankfully those aches don't last forever, but come and go without warning and at irregular intervals. Growth spurts normally coincide with the onset of puberty and can sometimes remain through adolescence; but the good news is; not always. Growth spurts generally are less common in girls.

The most common cure for growth spurts is to reduce training and competition, and in the most extreme cases, that's when it becomes too painful to run, complete rest. If in doubt the alternative is to seek professional advice; consulting a sports physio is usually the first step.

As in most things associated with the growth

and development of juniors there are no hard and fast rules. However, coaches, parents and importantly, the athletes themselves, have to pick their way through the maze of adolescence as a team. Once again, that's when communication is vital.

HILLS: Hill sessions should be included in every distance runners training schedule because uphill running creates physical and mental strength; it's through those strengths that speed develops and ultimately confidence. There is a knack to successful uphill running, especially as the hill steepens. It's then that the athlete shortens his/her stride, lifts the knees and pushes off the toes, while at the same time keeping the cadence high. The torso should be kept upright and the arms driven vigorously, while at the same time focusing on the top of the hill, because that's where they're heading for.

That's the hard work done, because once over the top everything changes. The stride lengthens to increase speed to maximum so as to distance the chasers, or conversely, to close the gap on those ahead; if there is anyone ahead. When running downhill throw caution to the wind, lean forward slightly and if necessary use the arms to stabilise balance; under no circumstances chop the stride or lean back; there's a risk of injury if they do, and the possible embarrassment of sitting down!

If possible, walk or drive the course before a race as it's the only way of knowing where the hills are, and more importantly their severity. Don't be frightened of hills, use them to your advantage.

INJURY: Injury is the word distance runners dread! There are aches and pains that experienced runners know they can run through, after a few minutes running they disappear. It is however, the ones that don't disappear that cause problems. In those cases the athlete must seek advice by speaking, as soon as possible, to a medical professional who ideally should be a sports physiotherapist; someone who comes recommended by a fellow athlete. The alternative is to consult a general practitioner who will usually arrange a referral to a hospital specialist; unfortunately that will probably mean joining a waiting list. Although the NHS. route is the cheaper of the two, a good sports physio is worth their weight in gold. Getting a quick consultation will save days, or even weeks of waiting in the queue for the NHS. In the case of all injuries, getting treatment fast is the main priority.

JOURNAL: The runner's journal, or training diary, is for recording daily running activities and also for planning future competition.

Training: when writing up daily training, record the following for future reference: how you felt, (before and after the run) the weather, the run itself and the route taken, the time the run took and the mileage. If it was a particular session log the details; ie:10 x 400m. 8 x hills and the splits. Another useful exercise is to record pulse rate: immediately after the run and then later at rest.

Competition: as with training: record all relevant details of races, don't skimp on detail.

Once fixtures are published, whether track, road or cross country, with your coach, make a note of the races that are important to you. Then plan in advance specific training with those races in mind.

Buying it: don't spend a fortune on a posh 'athletes' diary! Go to a discount stationery shop and buy a A5 hard back spiral bound one.

And finally: in these days of the smart phone it's common to log training electronically. Use both, with the phone as a back up, because if your phone is stolen or lost, so are your precious records.

KIT: There are no rules when it comes to buying or wearing kit, except that clothing should be comfortable and to a certain extent loose fitting, lycra and thermal base layers excepted.

Shoes: trainers, lightweight road racing shoes and spikes must always be at the top of the priority list for the obvious reasons. When buying them always use a reputable running shop where expert advice is on hand, preferably a runner. Try both shoes on, making sure they're flexible and comfortable. In the width there should be virtually no movement. In the length, there should be a gap of approximately one centimetre, no more, between the end of the big toe and the lining of the shoe. That gap allows for the expansion of the feet, especially during hot weather; and when buying shoes don't skimp on price. Wearing cheap shoes can cause foot abnormalities which will mean seeking specialist medical advice as soon as the problem occurs. In the short term it could mean the inconvenience of a few days off running, but if left too long, surgery; which will certainly mean more than a few days off!

Always keep toe nails cut short and take your own clean running socks when buying new shoes.

Winter clothing: always wear layers; starting with a lightweight long sleeve thermal vest as a base layer; layers trap warm air between them. The priority is to keep warm and dry and always being prepared for a sudden change in the weather; don't get caught out. If you're going to a training session warm up in your outer layers, peeling off only when you're fully warmed up, and as soon as the session is over get dressed quickly and warm down; not the other way round. After hard training muscles cool rapidly and must be allowed to return back to normal temperature gradually; which is why runners warm down. Warming down prevents any chemical waste in the blood, such as lactic acid, caused by the exercise, from forming, which causes soreness, stiffness and cramps.

Summer clothing: Don't over dress, whether training or racing. For competition, warm up in lightweight layers but discard them as soon as the body temperature rises.

If you're going for a training run of any distance, you'll soon warm up. There's nothing worse than having to peel off layers and carry them on the run, and don't tie clothing round the waist, it restricts movement, is uncomfortable and it's extra weight. Don't make a habit of carrying a water bottle otherwise you'll end up running lopsided. In the heat of summer, and knowing you're going to be running in it sooner or later, sip water during the day: practice it, you'll be doing yourself a favour.

When packing kit it's important, with the help of a long suffering parent to write a check list and lay all the kit out the night before, and take spare dry clothing. As well as shoes and clothing, take a bin liner (the bigger the better.) That's to sit on while you're changing shoes and struggling to get leggings or over trousers off just before the race start (especially at cross country) To save that struggle, and the ensuing panic, buy leggings or over trousers with zips in the outer leg; the longer the zip the better. That bin liner is especially useful as there's nothing more uncomfortable than starting the race with a wet or muddy backside. After the race, the multi-functional bin liner can be turned inside out and used to protect the car seat.

So the buzz words when buying and wearing kit are: Comfortable, Affordable and Practical.

LEG SPEED (CADENCE): Leg speed, or cadence, is the number of steps runners take when they're actually running. That number however, can sometimes depend on the race distance and the individual runner, but for distance runners the foot strike should be close to 180 a minute. A highly significant factor in sustaining cadence is the use of the arms. The faster the arms move the higher the cadence will be; arms govern leg speed, not legs, which is apparent when running up, or down, steep hills or when sprinting. Although 180 foot strikes a minute is the optimum leg speed, bear in mind that with many things in running, once again, there are no hard and fast rules regarding cadence because everyone's running styles, actions, and therefore cadence, is different.

MEDICATION: Doping controls operate at all levels in United Kingdom Athletics (UKA) as they do in governing bodies around the world. It is therefore, the responsibility of the individual athlete who takes regular medication to make sure that it's not on the list of banned substances; if in doubt contact UKA to check the list. The last thing a junior, or senior, athlete needs is to test positive at a race meeting and to be banned from competition through ignorance of the rules. If in doubt check it out.

NUTRIENT/NUTRITION: *Nutrient*: 'A substance that provides nourishment essential for the maintenance of life and for growth.' Reference: Concise Oxford Dictionary.

Nutrient is the fuel and nutrition is the way the nutrients are ingested and absorbed in to the body through a balanced daily diet. The needs of junior distance runners who, through the early years of physical growth and athletic development need that balance to be correct more than at any other time in their lives. When they've left home and no longer rely on mother's home cooking to sustain them then they're free to go down any dietary route they choose, but even then, and more importantly, they should still maintain the nutritional balance. Eat rubbish; run rubbish!

What drink? If it's coloured the chances are that it's full of additives, mainly sugar and other ingredients that are hard to pronounce, and don't drink excessive amounts of drinks that are high in caffeine either. These days, tap water is usually clean enough; especially if it's filtered. Milk is excellent, because it is high in protein, and in hot weather it's one of the best drinks for re-hydration.

There are of course, people who for various health reasons i.e. allergies etc. are unable to keep to the normal 'balanced' diet and rely on supplements for their necessary nutrients.

Whatever the needs of the individual regarding nutrition, the message is simple and the same for everyone: the engine can only achieve maximum performance when the correct fuel is used.

Always check the labels, and if the ingredients don't make sense; Google them.

OVER-TRAINING: The first sign of over-training is usually loss of form, staleness (which is a combination of lethargy and fatigue) and injury, but not necessarily in that order. The worst case scenario is if injury, especially if it's serious, occurs first and prevents junior runners, seniors too, from running. For the dedicated junior it can be a time of stress, which the experienced coach will recognise, and more importantly prevent from worsening, by using their mentoring and motivational skills. Getting the athlete back to physical fitness and mental well being is the top priority, and if that means adapting the schedule to prevent further over-training then it must be done; if only as a temporary measure.

PAIN: Pain is a by-product of distance running and I don't mean the pain associated with injury!

Scenario one: Imagine going for a 'variable pace' five km. run, starting at an easy 7 minute mileing, which most juniors in their mid to upper teens, who train regularly, can handle pain free. However, as the pace gradually increases to finish the run at 5 minute mileing, or faster, somewhere along the way it'll start hurting. It's that pain that is the by-product.

Scenario two: A group of juniors in the same age band are running a hill session comprising eight efforts with a walk/jog back recovery. They'll probably run the first effort pain free, but by the eighth they'll be on their knees. Distance runners learn how to manage pain in their own different way, but when it does kick in they should never back off; they must run through it.

Ultimately it's down to the development of mental strength and pain management. The most important thing to remember is that the pain doesn't last forever.

QUALITY OR QUANTITY?: Quality or quantity, which is the most important? One is no more important than the other, even for junior distance runners. Without quantity, that is running miles, juniors will never develop the stamina needed to go the race distance, whereas quality is about developing strength and speed.

Quantity: an eleven year old boy ran a 3k cross country league race in the u/13 age group for the first time. His only thought was to win, but he had to know he had the stamina to race that distance; he also had to have the confidence to win, he knew he has both; why? Because at one of his two weekly group training sessions he regularly ran for 30 minutes continuous. That continuous running, even at seven minute mileing pace means he ran way over the 3k race distance. In those sessions he has developed stamina, aerobic fitness, basic speed and most importantly, confidence.

In that cross country race he ran away from the field to win it from the front, despite running against boys much older and more physically developed than himself. The difference was his confident demeanour, he knew he had the stamina, strength and speed and the belief to win it from the front.

Quality: the same lad's second session of the week is speed based: 30 minutes, with the focus on quality. The efforts are not timed and the sessions vary from week to week. The group never know what the session is in advance, but they do know it'll be quality rather than quantity.

At weekends it's possible that same lad might be taking part in other sports, or, because he loves running so much, he could be competing in a young athlete's track meeting, a cross country race or a junior Park Run and let's not forget, as well as all that stuff he'll be doing PE at school.

And now a word of caution! As juniors improve they tend to believe more is best; which isn't necessarily the case. Encouraging them down the quantity route too soon is a recipe for disaster. A difficult, but important part of the coach's, and parents', role is preventing juniors from over-training... and over-racing.

RECOVERY: Recovery is one of the most important words in the athletes' vocabulary.

Whether it's recovering from a hard session, a tough race, an injury or illness, and there is no guide book governing the amount of recovery individuals need; everyone is different, some take longer than others.

The rule of thumb is: A runner should always listen to what their body is telling them.

STAMINA: (endurance): *Stamina*: 'The ability to sustain prolonged physical or mental effort' (Concise Oxford Dictionary).

As far as distance runners are concerned that definition says it all. By going that extra distance on a run, or doing the extra effort(s) in training will make all the difference, not only in developing stamina, but also to building confidence. As young athletes grow so does their strength, which means they can handle a steady increase in mileage and eventually incorporating a long steady run into the weekly training schedule; that long steady run is the foundation on which stamina is built.

Stamina is one of three all important 'S' words, along with Strength and Speed. All three are equally important in the development of the distance runner. Stamina and strength form the foundation on which speed is perfected through specific training sessions.

TRAINING: Training is a means to an end, whereas competition is an end to the means. Most coaches have their own ideas, opinions and methods regarding training, but must always remember that whatever methods they do adopt should be first and foremost for the benefit of the athlete. Consistent training is the key that opens the door to successful competition.

UNDERSTANDING: When there is something a junior athlete doesn't understand about anything to do with running, whether it's in a book or magazine, on television or video or even if it's a verbal instruction in a group session brief, then they must question it! Asking questions is the only way juniors will learn if they're not sure, and is something all coaches should actively encourage. And what's more, when a coach is asked a question, he, or she, must always answer it accurately and straightforwardly, but more importantly, in a way that doesn't embarrass the athlete, especially if it's in a group situation. The golden rule for the coach is; be coherent and don't waffle, and for the athlete, it's to listen, and if they're not sure; ask. And if they're still not sure, ask again.

VARIETY: There is a saying: 'Variety is the spice of life.' It's a saying that should be indelibly etched on every distance runner's brain, as should be: if it ain't broke don't fix it. Confused by the contradiction? Don't be! Because although most distance runners are generally creatures of habit, occasionally there are times when changes, especially changes to training can be beneficial. Repetitive training can sometimes be boring so mix it up now and again: occasionally try varying the track session; try fartlek off road; run out and back; do hill sessions; just try something different that's out of the normal comfort zone. There's nothing wrong with mixing and matching, especially if it does relieve boredom. A change can be as good as rest.......or even better?

WINNING: To win is the ultimate goal! Whether as an individual or as part of a team, it's a special feeling and everyone loves a winner.

'It's not the winning that's important it's the taking part.' heard that one? Try telling that to a talented junior who is used to winning, then wait for the reaction. Winning though, doesn't necessarily mean crossing the line first. In a race situation it's about pushing yourself as hard as you can, for as long as you can; hurting like you've never hurt before to achieve your goal. It's exactly the same in training, it's about giving that bit extra; and when you do, believe me, you'll feel great.

Winning is a state of mind, 'If you think you can't you never will, if you believe you can you will.' If you've given all there is to give, you've won your own private battle with yourself! That's winning.

X/COUNTRY: X/C running is by far and away the most efficient way of developing stamina, strength and speed, and applies to all distance runners, male, female, juniors, seniors and veterans......and above all, cross country is enjoyable.

When I was an active runner, after a winter of cross country running I was strong and ready for the months ahead, competing on the track and road, and as a coach I actively encourage all distance runners; not only juniors, to race cross country.

As well as racing cross country there are clear benefits to training on the country as well; because if you can run fast on grass and through mud and softer surfaces, try sand, you'll run fast on any surface.

There's a camaraderie like no other between cross country runners. Mud is good, and there are times when every one is covered in it at the end of the race. It's as if there's a fellowship; a common bond, between all club runners, young and old, from the elite up front, to the guys coming in at the back.

As well as the competition that exists between clubs and individuals, there is also a healthy rivalry between club mates as they battle for team and individual honours, and it doesn't matter at what level of competition they're running. Those rivalries usually start as juniors and evolve in to friendships, friendships that last well in to the years of senior competition.

YOUNG: Here's another saying: 'You're only young once,' and it's true, so enjoy your years as a junior with your friends, especially your running friends, because they're the ones you'll be sharing your athletic experiences with, and them theirs with you.

Other than the closeness of the immediate family, the most important part of the formative years will be to enjoy good health and success in education. Success at school, college and university is the key to unlocking the doors to a happy and fulfilling life. Along the way treat running not only as an enjoyable sport, but also as a way of 'stress busting' especially during periods of revision, exams and interviews, that's as well as everything that life throws at you as you build a career; and unless running is that career, it will only be part of your life, albeit a very enjoyable and significant part!

Z: Z is the last letter in my A 2 Z of distance running. Last is the word athletes don't want to hear, especially if it applies to them. It's where you don't want to be, but if you are don't worry because it's not the end of the world, although it might feel like it at the time. After all it's only a race!

Thank you for reading this book, I hope you enjoyed it.

APPENDIX

Mileage

The statistics below are taken over the actual weeks ran, or part of, and have been rounded down to the nearest half mile. The training diary for 1989 has been lost, probably collecting dust in an attic somewhere.

1979
Total mileage: 2091 over 48 weeks. Weekly average - 43.5. Highest week - 78

1980
Total mileage: 2936 over 52 weeks. Weekly average - 56.5 Highest week - 83

1981
Total mileage: 2657.5 over 50 weeks. Weekly average - 53 Highest week - 83

1982
Total mileage: 2972 over 52 weeks. Weekly average - 57 Highest week - 86

1983
Total mileage: 2817 over 52 weeks. Weekly average - 54 Highest week - 72

1984
Total mileage: 3228 over 52 weeks. Weekly average - 62 Highest week - 106

1985
Total mileage: 2829 over 52 weeks. Weekly average - 54.5 Highest week - 76.5

1986
Total mileage: 2141 over 50 weeks. Weekly average - 42.5 Highest week - 70 (Total weeks ran 50)

1987
Total mileage: 486 over 34 weeks. Weekly average - 14 Highest week - 57 (total weeks ran 34)

1988
Total mileage: 1246 over 45 weeks. Weekly average - 27.5 Highest week - 45 (Total weeks ran 45)

Grand Total: 23403.5 miles

PERSONAL BESTS

The following personal bests are for running the 'standard' distances on the track and road. In addition there were some 'non-standard' distances, for example 7.4 miles at Cheltenham and the Chichester to Portsmouth 25km as well as a number of road relays where the distances differed slightly year on year. If I had focused on one, or a couple of specific distances at a time instead of becoming the all round distance runner that I did become, then perhaps I'd have been able to have got those times down; but I didn't so I'll never know. No regrets, I loved running and did my best.

15 miles 1.25.55. Newport, May 1981

1500m. 4.20.3. High Wycombe, July1981

5 miles 26.14 Ruislip, February 1982

20 miles 1.57.00 Ruislip, April 1982

6 miles 31.46 Chalfont St. Peter, June 1982

5000m. 15.24 High Wycombe, July 1982

10000m. 34.41 Carn Brae, Cornwall, August 1982

10 miles 54.04 Reading, September 1983

Half marathon 70.13 Bath, March 1984

Marathon. 2.35.18 London, May 1984

3000m. 9.10.9. Spikes Bridge, July 1984

10k. (Road) 32.50 Harrow, April 1985

FURTHER READING

Julian Goater: The Art of Running Faster.

Arthur Lydiard & Garth Gilmour: Running with Lydiard.

Bruce Tulloh: The Teenage Runner.

John Bryant: The London Marathon. 3:59.4.

Charlie Spedding: From Last to First.

Sebastian Coe: The Winning Mind.

Harry Wilson: Running Dialogue-A Coach's Story.

Printed in Great Britain
by Amazon